The Awakening

AMIT BUTANI

notionpress.com

INDIA • SINGAPORE • MALAYSIA

TABLE OF CONTENTS

INTRODUCTION

Dear Reader,

Have you ever found yourself gazing up at the night sky, your mind filled with wonder as you ponder the vastness of the universe? Have you ever questioned the very essence of your being, yearning to decode the enigmatic secrets hidden within your soul? If so, then prepare yourself for an extraordinary journey of self-discovery unlike any other. Welcome to "The Awakening," a book that will take you on a transformative odyssey to unlock the mysteries of your own existence.

In these pages, we delve deep into the heart of the most profound question that has haunted humanity for centuries. Who are we? Where have we come from? And where will we go after we depart from this mortal coil? These existential queries have plagued philosophers, theologians, and seekers of truth throughout the ages. But fear not, dear reader, for within these very pages lies the key to unlocking the answers you seek.

But before we embark on this transformative expedition, allow me to introduce myself. My name is Amit Butani, and while my professional life has been immersed in the world of marketing and travel, my true passion lies in the realm of spiritual sciences. I stand before you as a humble student of the mysteries that lie beyond our comprehension, forever thirsting for knowledge and seeking to illuminate the path of enlightenment.

Within my being, I have discovered the delicate dance between the physical realm and the ethereal dimensions that exist beyond our mortal senses. I have spent countless hours exploring the realms of energy healing, seeking solace within the comforting embrace of aromatherapy, NLP, and meditative practices. My journey has taken me to the peaks of breathtaking mountains and the depths of my own consciousness, all in the pursuit of understanding the ineffable truths that lie within the human experience.

As I stand here today, ready to guide you on this transformative path, it is not as an enlightened guru or sage, but rather as a fellow traveler on the road to self-discovery. I bring to you my humble experiences and the wisdom I have gleaned on my own quest for truth. Together, we shall navigate the labyrinthine corridors of the soul in search of purpose, meaning, and the keys to unlock the door to our highest potential.

The journey that awaits you within these pages is one of profound self-exploration, a voyage that will challenge your perceptions and provoke your deepest thoughts. We shall embark on this odyssey armed with thought-provoking insights and practical exercises, designed to delve into the depths of your soul and uncover the hidden jewels that lay within.

Imagine, if you will, the feeling of stepping onto a gossamer path, guided by the soft whispers of the wind and the gentle melody of nature all around. Close your eyes for a moment, and envision the soft hues of a sunrise casting its gentle glow upon your face. Picture yourself standing at the precipice of a grand canyon, feeling the awe-inspiring power of the universe coursing through your veins. This is the journey that awaits you, dear reader, a journey of self-discovery that will leave you forever transformed.

As we traverse the landscapes of the mind, body, and spirit, we shall uncover the intricate tapestry of our true essence. We shall explore the depths of our being, shining a light upon the shadows that have veiled our understanding for far too long. Together, we shall unravel the secrets of the universe, discovering the purpose and meaning that will guide us on our path to fulfillment and enlightenment.

So, dear reader, I invite you to take my hand and embark upon this extraordinary adventure. Let us set forth on a quest for truth, guided by the whispers of the universe and the beating of our own hearts. Let us awaken to the boundless potential that lies within us all, for it is in this awakening that we shall find our true selves.

With open hearts and curious minds, let us begin our journey of self-discovery. Welcome to "The Awakening."

Yours in exploration,

Amit Butani

CHAPTER 1

THE AWAKENING

Who Are We?

The Origins of Humanity

To embark on this journey of discovery, I sought out various sources of knowledge and wisdom. Ancient texts, scientific research papers, and spiritual teachings were all part of my quest to unravel the secrets of our existence. I spent countless hours poring over books, attending lectures, and engaging in thought-provoking discussions.

One of the most enlightening perspectives I came across was the concept of the spiritual evolution of humanity. It posited that our species had undergone a gradual awakening throughout history, progressing from a state of pure instinct-driven survival to a more conscious and self-aware existence. This idea resonated with me deeply, as I could see the traces of this evolution within myself and the world around me.

My research led me to ancient civilizations that had flourished long before our modern era. The wisdom contained in texts such as the Vedas, the Upanishads, the Egyptian Book of the Dead, and the Sumerian tablets provided glimpses into the beliefs and ideologies of these ancient societies. I studied their creation myths, their understanding of the cosmos, and their concepts of divinity.

I delved into the works of philosophers such as Plato and Aristotle, who grappled with questions of existence and sought to understand the nature of the soul. Their perspectives allowed me to contemplate the interconnectedness of all life and the immortality of the soul.

Scientific research played a vital role in my exploration as well. The fields of anthropology, archaeology, and genetics provided valuable insights into the origins of humanity. Study after study revealed that we are all interconnected, sharing a common ancestry that dates back thousands of years. The discovery of ancient hominid fossils, the analysis of DNA, and the tracing of migration patterns all contributed to our understanding of who we are and where we come from.

As I gathered this vast array of information, I couldn't help but be overwhelmed by the grandeur of it all. It became apparent that our existence was not a mere accident, but rather a result of an intricate cosmic dance that stretched back billions of years. We were not isolated beings, but rather part of a vast interconnected web of life.

Contemplating our place in the universe, I realized that each one of us has a unique role to play in the grand scheme of things. Our experiences, both joyful and challenging, shape our souls and contribute to the evolution of consciousness. We are not mere spectators but active participants in the ongoing story of humanity.

In my own life, this realization brought a profound sense of purpose and responsibility. I understood that I had the power to shape my reality and contribute to the greater good. This newfound understanding propelled me to explore various healing modalities and spiritual practices. I became a certified life coach, learning techniques to empower others and guide them on their own journeys of self-discovery.

The more I immersed myself in these practices, the more I saw the interconnectedness of body, mind, and spirit. I realized that true well-being could only be achieved when all aspects of our being were in harmony. This insight led me to a deep exploration of the physical, mental, emotional, and spiritual levels of existence.

I studied the ancient science of Ayurveda, understanding how our bodies are composed of the elements of nature and how their balance affects our overall health. I learned about the power of energy healing, using methods such as Eden Energy Medicine and EFT/TFT to restore the flow of energy within the body. Aromatherapy became a part of my daily life, harnessing the healing properties of plants to support emotional and mental well-being.

Meditation became a cornerstone of my spiritual practice, allowing me to quiet the mind and tap into a deeper level of consciousness. I explored various breathing techniques, such as the Science of Life & Breath and the Wim Hof breathing technique, discovering the profound effects that breathwork has on our physical and mental states.

My journey of self-discovery and exploration continues to this day. I am constantly learning, growing, and evolving as I delve deeper into the mysteries of our existence. Through my studies and experiences, I have come to realize that life is a precious gift, and it is up to each of us to make the most of it. We have the power to shape our reality, to embrace our true potential, and to create a world that is filled with love, compassion, and harmony.

In writing this book, my aim is to share these insights and empower all who are willing to embark on their own journey of self-discovery. I invite you to join me in exploring the depths of your being, to awaken to your true potential, and to create a life that is aligned with your highest purpose. Together, let us unlock the mysteries of our existence and embrace the beauty and wonder of being human.

The Afterlife

One of the earliest recorded beliefs in the afterlife can be traced back to ancient Egypt. The Egyptians, renowned for their elaborate funeral rituals and elaborate tombs, believed in the concept of the soul's journey to the "Hall of Ma'at" after death. They believed that in order for the soul to continue its existence in the afterlife, it had to undergo a judgment where its heart was weighed against the Feather of Ma'at, symbolizing truth and justice. If the heart was found to be pure, the soul was granted eternal paradise, known as the Field of Reeds, where they would be reunited with their loved ones.

In contrast to this belief, ancient Greeks held a different perspective on the afterlife. Influenced by philosophical ideas, they believed in the existence of the Underworld, a realm ruled by Hades, the god of the dead. According to Greek mythology, the souls of the deceased would embark on a perilous journey to reach the Underworld. Once there, the soul would face judgment and be assigned to one of three fates: Elysium, a paradise reserved for the virtuous; Tartarus, a place of punishment for the wicked; or Asphodel Meadows, a mundane existence for those who lived unremarkable lives.

Moving forward in history, religious beliefs also played a significant role in shaping perspectives on the afterlife. In major religions like Christianity, Islam, and Hinduism, the concept of heaven and hell takes center stage. These religions emphasize the idea of rewards and punishments in the afterlife based on a person's deeds and faith during their earthly existence. While the specifics differ between these faiths, the underlying principle remains similar - the soul's eternal destination is determined by its behavior in the mortal realm.

Philosophers, too, have left a profound impact on the exploration of the afterlife. Ancient Greek philosophers such as Plato and Pythagoras contemplated the notion of the immortality of the soul. Plato's allegory of the cave is particularly insightful, suggesting that the physical world is a mere shadow of the true reality found in the world of the forms. According to Plato, the soul contains knowledge acquired in previous lives and longs to return to its divine origin.

In more recent times, scientific advancements have brought us closer to understanding the mysteries of life after death. Near-death experiences (NDEs) have been extensively studied and have provided intriguing insights into what may lie beyond the physical realm. Many individuals who have experienced an NDE report seeing a bright light, a feeling of peace and love, and a sense of detachment from their physical bodies. While skeptics argue that these experiences are merely the result of physiological processes in the brain, those who have undergone them maintain that there is an undeniable spiritual component.

Furthermore, advancements in the field of quantum physics have given rise to theories about the nature of consciousness and its potential survival beyond death. The concept of the multiverse, where multiple universes coexist simultaneously, opens up the possibility of alternate dimensions and realities where consciousness continues to exist. Quantum physicists propose that consciousness may transcend the physical body and be interconnected with a greater cosmic consciousness.

As I contemplate these various perspectives on the afterlife, I am struck by the common thread that runs through them all - the belief that there is something beyond our mortal existence. While the specifics and interpretations may vary, the fundamental longing for continuity and a deeper understanding of our existence persists.

Personally, I find solace in the idea of a multidimensional reality, where consciousness continues to evolve and expand. It aligns with my spiritual journey, which has been driven by a thirst for knowledge and a desire to explore the mystical unknown. My experiences with various healing modalities and practices have deepened my understanding of the interconnectedness of all things and the potential for growth beyond the physical plane.

In the end, I believe that the concept of life after death is a deeply personal and subjective one. It is shaped by our experiences, beliefs, and the yearnings of our souls. Whether we find comfort in the traditions of our ancestors, the teachings of religious faiths, or the mysteries of science, the exploration of the afterlife invites us to contemplate the larger questions of our existence. It encourages us to live our lives with intention, embracing the opportunity to grow and expand our consciousness while we have the gift of this human experience.

As I continue on my spiritual journey, I am reminded that the concept of life after death is not to be feared but embraced as a natural part of the cycle of existence. It invites us to lead purposeful lives, striving for growth, and deepening our connection to the divine. Ultimately, it reminds us that life is a precious gift, and it is our responsibility to make the most of it while we are here.

Seeking Meaning

But what exactly does it mean to find meaning in life? Is it about achieving success and recognition? Is it about accumulating wealth and material possessions? Or is there something more profound at play?

For me, the journey of seeking meaning began when I was introduced to the world of spirituality and metaphysics. As a marketing professional in the travel retail industry, I spent most of my days immersed in the fast-paced corporate world. While I enjoyed my work and the challenges it brought, there always lingered a sense of emptiness within me. I yearned for something deeper, something that would nourish my soul.

It was during this phase of my life that I stumbled upon the study of spiritual sciences. I delved into the realms of energy healing, mindfulness, and personal development. As I embarked on this new path, I realized that the search for meaning is not about external achievements or possessions. Instead, it is about delving into the depths of our being and discovering our true essence.

Finding meaning in life is a journey of self-discovery. It is about uncovering our passions, values, and purpose. It requires us to question the beliefs and societal conditioning that have shaped our lives. It demands that we confront our fears and limitations, and embrace the fullness of who we are.

It is through this process of self-exploration that we begin to understand our unique gifts and talents. We start to recognize the activities and pursuits that ignite a spark within us that make us come alive. For me, this realization came in the form of my love for the mystical unknown. I yearned to understand the deeper mysteries of life and to explore the realms of consciousness.

But seeking meaning goes beyond just discovering our passions and interests. It also involves aligning our actions and choices with our core values. It requires us to live in integrity and authenticity, to embody the qualities and virtues that resonate with our true essence.

When we live a life of purpose and meaning, we experience a profound sense of fulfillment. We find joy in what we do, and our actions become infused with a sense of purpose. We no longer feel like mere spectators in our own lives, but active participants in the creation of our destiny.

But why is finding meaning so important? What does it truly offer us?

First and foremost, meaning gives us a sense of direction. It provides us with a compass to navigate the twists and turns of life. When we have a clear sense of purpose, we can make choices that are aligned with our values and aspirations. We can set goals and work towards achieving them, knowing that we are moving towards a greater purpose.

Furthermore, meaning offers us a sense of fulfillment. When we engage in activities that resonate with our true essence, we tap into a wellspring of joy and satisfaction. We no longer feel the need to seek validation or approval from others, as our actions are born out of our own authentic expression.

Seeking meaning also cultivates a deeper sense of connection and belonging. As we explore our own inner landscape, we begin to recognize the interconnectedness of all beings. We understand that we are part of something greater, and that our actions have a ripple effect on the world around us. This realization fosters a sense of compassion and empathy, as we seek to uplift and support others in their own journey of self-discovery.

Ultimately, finding meaning in life is about reclaiming our power and taking ownership of our own happiness. It is about recognizing that we have the ability to shape our reality and create a life of purpose and fulfillment. It is an invitation to step into our true potential and to live life to its fullest.

As I continue on my own journey of seeking meaning, I am reminded of the words of Viktor Frankl, the renowned psychiatrist and Holocaust survivor: "The meaning of life is to give life meaning." This simple yet profound statement encapsulates the essence of what it means to seek meaning. It is a reminder that our lives hold immense potential and purpose, and it is up to us to uncover and embrace it.

In conclusion, the search for meaning is a deeply personal and transformative journey. It is a quest that requires courage, curiosity, and a willingness to challenge our own assumptions and beliefs. But amidst the uncertainties and complexities of life, finding meaning is a beacon of light that guides us towards a life of purpose, fulfillment, and joy.

Embracing Change

In my journey of self-discovery and spiritual awakening, I have come to realize the profound impact that change can have on our lives. Change shakes us out of our complacency, pushes us out of our comfort zones, and forces us to confront the edges of our existence. It is through change that we truly learn and grow.

But why is change so difficult for many of us? Perhaps it is because we fear the unknown, the uncertainty that comes with stepping into uncharted territory. We cling onto what is familiar, even if it no longer serves us, because the prospect of change feels overwhelming.

However, it is in those moments of discomfort and unease that we have the greatest opportunity for growth. Change challenges us to adapt, to evolve, and to become the best versions of ourselves. It is through change that we shed our old ways of being and open ourselves up to new possibilities.

I believe that change is not a random occurrence, but rather a lesson and a gift from the universe. It is through change that we are given the chance to redefine ourselves, to shed old beliefs and patterns that no longer serve us, and to embrace a new way of being.

But how do we embrace change? How do we shift our perspective from one of fear and resistance to one of openness and acceptance? It begins with a willingness to let go of what no longer serves us and a commitment to personal growth.

For me, embracing change has been an ongoing journey. As a marketing professional in the travel retail industry, I have witnessed firsthand the power of change in the business world. Market trends shift, consumer behaviors change, and it is our ability to adapt and innovate that determines our success.

In my personal life, change has also played a significant role. I met my soulmate at a young age, and together we have built a beautiful life and family. But even in the midst of this stability, I have been drawn to the study of spiritual sciences and healing modalities. The thirst for knowledge and growth has led me to explore various practices, each one contributing to my own personal transformation.

I have delved into the realm of energy medicine, becoming a certified life coach and practitioner of Eden energy medicine. I have learned the power of breathwork, undertaking various courses and becoming an active breath practitioner. I have explored the depths of my mind through meditation and NLP, and have even tapped into the healing properties of aromatherapy.

Through these experiences, I have come to understand that change is not something to be feared, but rather embraced. It is through change that we learn about ourselves, about our strengths and weaknesses, and about the infinite potential that lies within us.

But embracing change does not mean that we become passive observers in our own lives. It requires active engagement, a willingness to take risks and step outside of our comfort zones. It requires us to examine our belief systems, to question our assumptions, and to challenge the status quo.

The role of change in our lives is not simply limited to personal growth and transformation. It extends to every facet of our existence, from our physical bodies to our relationships, our careers, and our connection to the world around us.

Change is the driving force behind innovation and progress. It is through change that we are able to adapt to new circumstances, to overcome obstacles, and to reach our highest potential. Without change, we would remain stagnant, trapped in a never-ending cycle of sameness.

So how do we begin to embrace change? It starts with a shift in mindset, a conscious decision to view change not as a threat, but as an opportunity. It requires us to let go of the need for control and certainty, and to trust in the process of life.

But it is important to remember that embracing change does not mean that we have to abandon everything we know. It is about finding a balance between holding onto what anchors us and stepping into the unknown. It is about honoring where we have come from while being open to the possibilities of where we can go.

Change is the catalyst for growth and transformation. It is the key to unlocking our fullest potential and living a life of purpose and fulfillment. So let us embrace change with open arms, knowing that it is through change that we truly awaken and become the best versions of ourselves.

The Power of Intuition

Exploring the intuitive wisdom within is the first step towards harnessing this power. It requires us to go beyond the realm of the mind and connect with our true essence, our higher self. This connection is not limited to a select few; rather, it is something that is available to each and every one of us. It is a matter of acknowledging its existence and being open to its guidance.

One of the ways in which I began to tap into my intuitive wisdom was through meditation. By quieting the mind and creating a space of stillness, I was able to connect with a deeper part of myself. Sitting in silence, focusing on my breath, and allowing thoughts to pass through without attachment, I began to experience moments of clarity and insight. It was in these moments that I realized the power of my intuition.

Another technique I found helpful was journaling. Writing down my thoughts and feelings without judgment or analysis allowed me to tap into a deeper level of self-awareness. It was through this practice that I began to notice patterns, themes, and recurring symbols that held significance for me. I discovered that my intuition often communicated with me through symbols and signs, guiding me towards the right path or warning me of potential pitfalls.

In addition to meditation and journaling, I found that connecting with nature played a pivotal role in developing my intuition. Nature has a way of grounding and calming our minds, allowing us to become more present and receptive to the subtle messages around us. Whether it was taking long walks in the forest or simply sitting by the ocean, I felt a deep connection with the natural world. It was during these moments of communion with nature that my intuitive senses sharpened, and I became more attuned to the energy and vibrations that surrounded me.

As I continued to explore and embrace my intuition, I realized that it had a profound impact on my decision-making process. It guided me towards choices that were aligned with my true purpose and brought me a sense of fulfillment and joy. Rather than relying solely on my logical mind, I learned to trust the wisdom of my intuition. It became a guiding force in my life, helping me navigate through the complexities and challenges that came my way.

One of the most fascinating aspects of intuition is that it is not limited to our personal experiences or knowledge.

It has the ability to tap into a universal wisdom, a collective consciousness that transcends time and space. It is through this connection that we can access insights and guidance that go beyond our limited perspective. In moments of stillness and openness, we can tap into this vast reservoir of wisdom, allowing it to inform our decision-making and shape our lives.

However, harnessing the power of intuition does not mean disregarding logic and rational thinking. Instead, it is about finding a balance between the two. Our rational mind is valuable in gathering information, analyzing facts, and making calculated decisions. But when it comes to matters of the heart, matters of the soul, intuition often knows best. It has the ability to sense the underlying truth, beyond what the mind can comprehend.

Learning to trust our intuition takes time and practice. It requires us to let go of our need for certainty and control, and instead, surrender to the unknown. It is a process of unlearning, of shedding the layers of conditioning and societal expectations that have clouded our intuitive senses. But as we embark on this journey of self-discovery, we open ourselves up to a world of infinite possibilities and deep inner knowing.

In this fast-paced, information-driven world, where we often find ourselves overwhelmed by choices and decisions, our intuition can serve as a guiding light. It is a source of wisdom that lies within each and every one of us, waiting to be discovered and embraced. By embracing our intuition, we empower ourselves to make decisions that are aligned with our higher purpose and bring a sense of fulfillment and joy into our lives.

So I invite you on this journey of self-discovery and empowerment. I invite you to explore the intuitive wisdom within, to connect with your higher self, and tap into the vast reservoir of knowledge that lies beyond the realm of the mind. Trust in your intuition, for it knows the way, even when your logical mind may be clouded by doubt. And as you delve deeper into the realm of intuition, you will find a sense of clarity, purpose, and alignment that transcends the limitations of the physical world.

Cultivating Self-Awareness

Self-awareness, a concept that has been explored by philosophers, psychologists, and spiritual teachers for centuries, refers to the ability to observe and understand oneself in a deep and meaningful way. It is the foundation of personal growth and transformation, allowing individuals to gain insights into their thoughts, emotions, behaviors, and motivations. By cultivating self-awareness, individuals become more conscious of their strengths, weaknesses, values, and beliefs, leading to better decision-making, healthier relationships, and a greater sense of purpose in life.

In today's fast-paced and digitally-driven world, it can be easy to lose touch with oneself amidst the constant distractions and demands of daily life. Many people find themselves caught up in the endless cycle of work, family responsibilities, and social obligations, neglecting their own needs and desires in the process. Without self-awareness, we become disconnected from our true selves, living on autopilot and unable to tap into our full potential.

Discover the Importance of Self-Awareness:

The journey of self-awareness begins with a simple but profound realization – that we are not our thoughts, emotions, or external circumstances. The true essence of who we are lies deeper within, beyond the surface-level identifications with our roles, achievements, and material possessions. It is through self-awareness that we can start to uncover this hidden wisdom within ourselves.

Self-awareness allows us to step back from the constant stream of thoughts and emotions, and observe them with a sense of detachment. We begin to notice patterns, triggers, and habits that may have been previously unconscious. This awareness shines a light on our self-sabotaging behaviors, limiting beliefs, and negative thought patterns, empowering us to make conscious choices and break free from self-imposed limitations.

Furthermore, self-awareness opens the door to self-acceptance and self-compassion. As we become more intimately acquainted with our thoughts and emotions, we develop a greater understanding and empathy towards ourselves. We realize that all aspects of ourselves, even the less desirable ones, are a part of our unique human experience. This acceptance allows us to show kindness and compassion towards ourselves, fostering a nurturing inner environment that supports personal growth and well-being.

Practical Techniques to Cultivate Self-Awareness:

Cultivating self-awareness is not a journey that can be achieved overnight. It requires consistent effort, patience, and a willingness to explore the depths of our being. There are various techniques and practices that can aid in this process, each offering unique perspectives and tools to deepen self-awareness.

1. Mindfulness Meditation: Mindfulness meditation is a powerful practice that involves intentionally paying attention to the present moment without judgment. By focusing on our breath, bodily sensations, thoughts, and emotions, we begin to develop an observing awareness that transcends our usual identification with them. Regular mindfulness meditation helps cultivate a calm and clear mind, allowing us to tune into our inner wisdom and gain insights into our true nature.

2. Journaling: Writing our thoughts and feelings in a journal can be a valuable tool for self-reflection and self-discovery. By putting our experiences into words, we can gain clarity and gain a different perspective on our thoughts and emotions. Journaling provides a safe space for expressing and processing our thoughts and feelings, enabling us to uncover underlying patterns or beliefs that may be influencing our behaviors.

3. Self-Reflection Exercises: Engaging in self-reflection exercises, such as asking ourselves thought-provoking questions or analyzing our past

experiences, can help deepen our understanding of ourselves. These exercises prompt us to explore our values, beliefs, strengths, and areas for growth. By reflecting on our experiences, we can uncover valuable insights that inform our decisions and actions in the present.

4. Seeking Feedback: Inviting feedback from trusted friends, family members, or mentors can provide a valuable external perspective on our behaviors and qualities. Others may notice patterns or blind spots that we are unaware of, offering us an opportunity to grow and evolve. Being open to feedback and genuinely considering it allows us to expand our self-awareness and become more in tune with our impact on others.

5. Body-Mind Connection: Cultivating self-awareness involves a holistic approach that includes not just the mind but the body as well. Practices such as yoga, tai chi, or body scan meditations help us develop a deeper connection with our physical sensations, breath, and energy. By tuning into our body, we can better understand the signals it provides and make conscious choices that support our well-being.

Conclusion:

Cultivating self-awareness is a transformative journey that leads to personal growth, self-acceptance, and a richer, more purposeful life. By dedicating time and effort to observe ourselves with kindness and curiosity, we unlock the power to choose how we engage with ourselves and the world around us. Through practices like mindfulness meditation, journaling, self-reflection, seeking feedback, and nurturing the body-mind connection, we can deepen our understanding of ourselves and embrace the innate wisdom that resides within us. As we embark on this journey of self-awareness, we empower ourselves to live authentically, joyfully, and in alignment with our true nature.

Embracing the Unknown

The journey of embracing the unknown begins with a simple yet provocative question – what if? What if we let go of our fears and limitations? What if we open ourselves up to the vast expanse of possibilities that stretch before us? It is through curiosity and openness that we can truly navigate the uncharted territories of life.

For me, this journey of embracing the unknown began many years ago. Growing up in a traditional Indian household, the focus was always on stability and security. Going against the grain, I found solace in the study of spiritual sciences. While my professional life revolved around marketing and finance, my soul yearned for something deeper – a connection to the mystical unknown.

It was during my years in the UK, pursuing my MBA, that I stumbled upon the fascinating world of healing modalities. Energy medicine, life coaching, aromatherapy

– these were not just tools to heal others, but a means to delve into the depths of my own being. I became a certified practitioner later on in life in various techniques, constantly thirsting for more knowledge and understanding.

The more I delved into these practices, the more I realized that embracing the unknown was not about finding all the answers. It was about having the courage to ask the questions and explore the realms of the unexplored. It was about acknowledging that we are all works in progress, forever evolving and growing.

To satisfy my thirst for knowledge, I immersed myself in various breathing techniques. The Science of Life & Breath, Dopamine Activated Breathing, Transcendental Meditation Breath Work – these courses taught me the power of breath as a tool for transformation. Through these practices, I learned to navigate the unknown territories of my own mind and tap into the immense power within.

But embracing the unknown is not just about internal exploration. It is about immersing oneself in the wonders of the external world as well. Nature became my sanctuary, my place of solace and inspiration. I would often find myself lost in the lush green forests, surrounded by the symphony of birdsong and the gentle rustle of leaves. It is in these moments of connection with the natural world that I truly felt alive.

Trekking and hiking became a way for me to challenge myself physically, mentally, and emotionally. The mountains, with their towering peaks and treacherous paths, taught me the value of perseverance and determination. The unknown trails ahead became a metaphor for the unknown territories of life, each step a lesson in trust and surrender.

In the midst of this journey, I found my soulmate. Our love story began when she was just 14, and I was 16. Since then, we have grown together, supporting each other through the ups and downs of life. Our love has been a constant source of strength and inspiration, reminding me of the power of connection and the beauty of shared experiences.

As a father of two beautiful children, the responsibility to embrace the unknown takes on a new meaning. I strive to be an example for them – to show them that there is beauty in the unknown, and that true growth comes from stepping outside of our comfort zones. Together, we explore the mysteries of life, igniting their curiosity and nurturing their sense of wonder.

Through all these experiences and practices, I have come to realize that embracing the unknown is not about finding all the answers, but about developing a mindset of curiosity and openness. It is about acknowledging that life is unpredictable, and that the greatest adventures lie in the uncharted territories.

So, as I journey through the pages of this book, I invite you to join me in embracing the unknown. Let us release our fears and limitations, and step into a world of endless possibilities. Let us explore the depths of our own being, surrendering to the mysteries of life. Together, let us navigate the unknown with curiosity and openness, for it is within this embrace that we truly awaken to the magic that surrounds us.

CHAPTER 2

THE ESSENCE OF BEING

Exploring Inner Wisdom

The exploration of inner wisdom is a journey that takes us beyond the realm of our physical existence and into the depths of our soul. It is a quest that requires us to shed our ego and surrender to the whispers of our inner being. Through this connection, we tap into a wellspring of knowledge and insight that has been lying dormant within us all along.

In the hustle and bustle of everyday life, it is easy to become disconnected from our true selves. We get caught up in the external world, constantly seeking validation and approval from others. We become slaves to society's expectations, sacrificing our own desires and dreams in the process. We lose touch with our inner wisdom, the voice that knows what is truly best for us.

But deep within us, there is a wellspring of guidance waiting to be discovered. Our inner wisdom is like a compass, always pointing us in the right direction. It knows our true purpose and desires, and it holds the key to unlocking our fullest potential.

To dive into the depths of our being and connect with our inner wisdom, we must first learn to quiet the noise of the external world. We must create space for stillness and silence, allowing our inner voice to be heard. This can be achieved through practices such as meditation, breathwork, and spending time in nature.

Meditation is a powerful tool for accessing our inner wisdom. By sitting in stillness and observing our thoughts, we can begin to separate ourselves from the constant chatter of the mind. As we cultivate a sense of detachment, we create space for our inner wisdom to emerge. It is in these moments of silence that we can hear the whispers of our soul.

Breathwork is another technique that can help us dive deep within ourselves. Through conscious and intentional breathing, we can release tension and stagnant energy that may be blocking our connection to our inner wisdom. By bringing awareness to our breath, we can tap into our body's innate intelligence and wisdom.

Spending time in nature is also essential for reconnecting with our inner wisdom. Nature has a way of grounding us and reminding us of our place in the grand scheme of things. As we immerse ourselves in the beauty of the natural world, we are reminded of the interconnectedness of all things. Nature holds a mirror to our inner selves and allows us to see the beauty and wisdom within.

Once we have created the space for inner wisdom to emerge, we must also learn to trust it. Trusting our inner wisdom requires us to let go of our need for external validation and approval. It requires us to have the courage to follow our own path, even when it goes against the expectations of others.

Trusting our inner wisdom also means being willing to make mistakes and learn from them. Our inner wisdom is not infallible, but it is always guiding us towards growth and expansion. It knows that the path to enlightenment is not a straight line but a winding journey filled with twists and turns. It is through our mistakes and failures that we learn the most valuable lessons and come closer to realizing our true potential.

As we dive into the depths of our being and connect with our inner wisdom, we become co-creators of our own reality. We no longer rely on external circumstances to dictate our happiness and fulfillment. We take responsibility for our own well-being on all levels of existence – physical, mental, emotional, and spiritual.

Connecting with our inner wisdom allows us to tap into a source of unlimited potential and power. It enables us to make decisions from a place of inner knowing and clarity. It opens up a whole new world of possibilities and allows us to live life to the fullest.

So, I invite you to dive into the depths of your being and connect with your inner wisdom and intuition. Embrace the journey of self-discovery and self-empowerment. Trust that within you lies a wellspring of knowledge and insight waiting to be unleashed. Believe in your own greatness and the unlimited potential that resides within you. With every step you take towards self-discovery, know that you are one step closer to awakening the true power that lies dormant within.

Embrace the unknown, and let your inner wisdom be your guiding light.

The Power of Self-Reflection

As I sat on the sandy beach, watching the waves crashing against the shore, I couldn't help but wonder about the incredible power of self-reflection. It was a serene moment, a rare opportunity to be alone with my thoughts and delve into the depths of my being. The sound of the waves served as a backdrop to my contemplation, its rhythmic nature soothing my restless mind.

Self-reflection had become an integral part of my daily routine. It was through this practice that I began to unravel the mysteries of my own existence and embark on a journey of self-discovery and personal growth. I had come to realize that by taking the time to reflect on my thoughts, emotions, and actions, I was able to gain a deeper understanding of myself and make informed decisions about my life.

The process of self-reflection can be likened to peering into a mirror. It allows us to see ourselves as we truly are, flaws and all. It is not an easy task, for it requires a certain level of honesty and vulnerability. We must be willing to confront our shortcomings and acknowledge our mistakes. But in doing so, we open ourselves up to the possibility of growth and transformation.

One of the most valuable lessons I learned through self-reflection is the importance of taking responsibility for my own life. It is easy to blame external circumstances or other people for our unhappiness or lack of success. But the truth is, we have the power to shape our own destiny. By looking inward, we can identify the limiting beliefs and self-sabotaging patterns that may be holding us back. Only then can we begin to take the necessary steps to change our lives for the better.

Self-reflection also allows us to gain clarity and perspective. In the hustle and bustle of everyday life, it is all too easy to get caught up in the chaos and lose sight of what truly matters. By taking a step back and reflecting on our goals, values, and priorities, we can make more informed decisions and align our actions with our deepest desires.

Through self-reflection, I discovered the untapped potential within myself. I realized that I possessed talents and strengths that I had not fully utilized. By understanding my own capabilities, I was able to set meaningful goals and work towards realizing my full potential. Self-reflection also helped me identify areas for improvement and develop strategies to overcome my weaknesses.

But self-reflection is not just about looking inward; it is also about connecting with something greater than ourselves. As I explored the depths of my own being, I found a profound sense of connection to the universe and all living beings. I realized that we are all interconnected, and our actions have a ripple effect that extends far beyond ourselves.

The practice of self-reflection, I discovered, is not limited to quiet moments of solitude. It can be integrated into our daily lives, allowing us to maintain a sense of mindfulness and presence in every moment. By cultivating awareness of our thoughts, emotions, and actions, we can make conscious choices and live with intention.

As I continue to explore the power of self-reflection, I am filled with a sense of wonder and gratitude. I am grateful for the opportunity to delve into the depths of my own being and uncover the hidden truths that lay dormant within me. I am grateful for the lessons I have learned and the growth I have experienced. And I am grateful for the chance to share my journey with others, in the hope that they too may find empowerment and fulfillment through self-reflection.

In conclusion, self-reflection is a powerful tool that can lead to self-discovery and personal growth. It allows us to gain a deeper understanding of ourselves, take responsibility for our lives, and make informed decisions. It helps us gain clarity and perspective, tap into our untapped potential, and connect with something greater than ourselves. By cultivating the practice of self-reflection, we can navigate the complexities of life with grace and authenticity. So, I invite you to embark on this journey of self-discovery and embrace the transformative power of self-reflection.

Embracing Vulnerability

Embracing vulnerability requires opening oneself up to the possibility of being seen and known for who we truly are. It requires us to let go of our masks and defenses, to be willing to be seen in our imperfect and raw state. It is in this rawness, this unfiltered authenticity, that we actually create a space for genuine connection and intimacy.

I remember a pivotal moment in my own journey of embracing vulnerability. It was during a quantum healing therapy session when my therapist encouraged me to speak openly and honestly about my deepest fears and insecurities. At first, I resisted, feeling a sense of shame in revealing these aspects of myself. But as I began to share, I realized that there was a profound release in being heard and understood in my vulnerability. It was as if a weight had been lifted off my shoulders, and I felt a deep sense of connection with my therapist.

Through this experience, I came to understand that vulnerability is not weakness, but rather strength. It takes immense courage to be vulnerable, to expose our true selves to others. It is in this act of courage that we create the space for others to do the same. When we show up authentically, it gives permission for others to let down their guards and be themselves.

In our modern world, where social media and online personas have become the norm, vulnerability is often overlooked. We put forth carefully curated versions of ourselves, showcasing only the highlights and hiding our vulnerabilities. But in doing so, we create a façade that disconnects us from others and ourselves. We miss out on the depth and richness of intimate connections that can only be forged through vulnerability.

By embracing vulnerability, we allow ourselves to be seen in our entirety, our strengths and weaknesses alike. We create a space for empathy, understanding, and compassion to flow. No longer are we hiding behind masks, but rather we are standing in our truth, owning our stories, and inviting others to do the same.

Embracing vulnerability is not without its challenges. It requires us to face our deepest fears and insecurities head-on. It can feel uncomfortable and scary to expose ourselves in this way. But it is in this discomfort that true growth and transformation occur. It is through facing our fears that we find the freedom to be authentic and to connect with others on a profound level.

As I have embraced vulnerability in my own life, I have witnessed the power it holds in creating meaningful connections. It has taught me the importance of listening without judgment, of holding space for others to share their truth. It has deepened my relationships and allowed for a level of intimacy I had previously only dreamed of.

In order to fully embrace vulnerability, we must also cultivate self-compassion. We must learn to embrace our own imperfections and accept ourselves as we are. By showing ourselves kindness and understanding, we create a foundation of self-love that allows us to be vulnerable without fear of judgment or rejection.

Each time I allow myself to be vulnerable, I am reminded of the beauty and strength that lie in our shared humanity. We are all imperfect, flawed beings navigating this complex journey of life. When we embrace vulnerability, we invite others to do the same, creating a ripple effect of authenticity and connection.

In conclusion, embracing vulnerability is not easy, but it is a necessary step on the path to self-discovery and authentic connections. It requires courage, self-compassion, and a willingness to face our deepest fears. But the rewards are countless - deep connections, personal growth, and a sense of true authenticity. So, I encourage you to take that leap, to embrace vulnerability, and to experience the transformative power it holds.

The Beauty of Imperfection

From a young age, I was conditioned to believe that perfection equates to success. It was ingrained in me that I needed to strive for flawless grades, a perfect body, and an impeccable reputation. Society's definition of perfection was set in stone, and there was no room for deviation. But as I grew older and wiser, I began to question this notion.

It was during my personal journey through the realm of spiritual sciences that I discovered the beauty of imperfection. I realized that the pursuit of perfection is not only futile but also detrimental to one's well-being. It creates unnecessary pressure and anxiety, constantly pushing us to be someone we are not. It robs us of our authenticity and prevents us from fully embracing our flaws as an integral part of our unique journey.

Instead of striving for perfection, I choose to appreciate the beauty of imperfection. I believe that our flaws and quirks are what make us interesting and relatable. They are the raw and unfiltered aspects of our being that connect us to others on a deeper level. It is in our imperfections that we find strength, resilience, and character.

Embracing my own flaws has been a transformative experience. Growing up, I always felt self-conscious about my introverted nature. I constantly compared myself to my extroverted peers, feeling inadequate and out of place. But as I delved into the study of spiritual sciences, I began to understand that being introverted was not a flaw but a unique aspect of my personality. It allowed me to be introspective, empathetic, and deeply in tune with my thoughts and emotions. It was my introversion that led me to explore the mystical unknown and discover a world of healing modalities that have shaped my journey to this day.

Every flaw, every imperfection, and every misstep along the way has shaped me into the person I am today. They have guided me on a path of self-discovery and personal growth. I have learned to celebrate my flaws as badges of honor, symbols of my resilience and authenticity. They remind me that life is not always about the destination but rather the journey itself.

The beauty of imperfection lies in its ability to teach us valuable life lessons. It teaches us humility and reminds us that we are all human, prone to mistakes and imperfections. It teaches us compassion, both towards ourselves and others, as we learn to accept and embrace our flaws without judgment. It teaches us gratitude, as we realize that every flaw is an opportunity for growth and self-improvement. It teaches us resilience, as we learn to pick ourselves up after falling and continue on our unique journey with renewed strength and determination.

I urge you, dear reader, to embrace your flaws as a part of your unique journey. Appreciate the beauty in imperfection and understand that perfection is an illusion. There is no such thing as a flawless human being, for it is our flaws that make us beautifully imperfect. Embrace them, celebrate them, and use them as stepping stones towards self-discovery and personal growth.

Remember, it is in our imperfections that we find our true essence. It is through our flaws that we connect with others on a profound level. So, let go of the pressure to be perfect and instead focus on embracing your flaws. Embrace them as the colorful brushstrokes that paint the canvas of your life and create a beautiful masterpiece that is uniquely yours.

In doing so, you will unleash the power that lies within you – the power to be unapologetically yourself, flaws and all. Embrace your imperfections, for they are the keys to unlocking your true potential and living a life that is authentic, fulfilling, and meaningful.

Embodying Authenticity

As I embarked on my journey of self-discovery and spiritual awakening, one of the most profound lessons I learned was the significance of embodying authenticity. To truly live a fulfilling life, it is essential to be true to oneself and express our unique essence in the world.

Throughout history, there have been countless individuals who have embraced authenticity and left an indelible mark on society. From artists and writers to spiritual leaders and entrepreneurs, these trailblazers have shown us the power of embracing our true selves. They have dared to break free from societal norms and expectations, choosing instead to follow their own path, no matter how unconventional it may seem.

When we embody authenticity, we are not conforming to the expectations of others; instead, we are embracing our own truth. We understand that our worthiness and value come from within and are not dependent on external validation. Living authentically means being honest with ourselves and others about who we truly are, as well as honoring our own needs, desires, and values. It is about embracing our strengths and weaknesses and embracing the unique gifts and talents we bring to the world.

One of the greatest challenges we face in our quest for authenticity is overcoming the fear of judgment and rejection. Society often expects us to fit into predefined boxes, conforming to a set of standards and norms that may not align with our true selves. We fear that if we deviate from these expectations, we will be criticized, ostracized, or deemed unworthy. However, it is when we allow these fears to hold us back that we end up feeling empty, unfulfilled, and disconnected from our true selves.

Living authentically requires courage and vulnerability. It means having the strength to be true to ourselves even in the face of adversity. It means letting go of the need for external validation and instead seeking validation from within. When we embody authenticity, we find a sense of liberation and freedom that cannot be found by conforming to societal expectations. We become the architects of our own lives and the masters of our own destiny.

Expressing our true selves is not only important for our own well-being, but it also has a profound impact on those around us. When we live authentically, we give others permission to do the same. Our authenticity becomes a catalyst for personal growth and transformation, inspiring others to embrace their own unique qualities and live their lives to the fullest. It creates a ripple effect of self-discovery and empowerment that spreads far beyond ourselves.

Living authentically also brings a sense of alignment and harmony to our lives. When we are in alignment with our true selves, we experience a deep sense of inner peace and fulfillment. We no longer feel like we are living a double life, wearing masks to fit into various roles and personas. Instead, we are able to integrate all aspects of ourselves and live in congruence with our values and beliefs. This sense of alignment allows us to tap into our full potential and live our lives in a way that is authentic, purposeful, and meaningful.

In my own journey towards authenticity, I have discovered various practices and modalities that have helped me align with my true self. From meditation and breathwork to energy healing and personal development, these tools have enabled me to shed the layers of conditioning and societal expectations and embrace my authentic self. They have allowed me to tap into my intuition, connect with my higher self, and deepen my understanding of who I truly am.

As I continue to walk this path of self-discovery and spiritual awakening, I am reminded that authenticity is not a destination; it is a continuous journey. It requires ongoing self-reflection, self-awareness, and self-compassion. It requires us to constantly question and challenge the beliefs and patterns that no longer serve us. It requires us to be willing to step outside of our comfort zones and embrace the unknown.

Living authentically is not always easy, but the rewards far outweigh the challenges. It is a choice to live a life that is true to our hearts and souls, a life that is filled with purpose, happiness, and fulfillment. It is a choice to be the best version of ourselves, embracing our flaws and imperfections, and celebrating our uniqueness. It is a choice to live a life that is authentically ours.

Cultivating Self-Love

I believe that one of the most powerful journeys we can embark on is the journey to self-love. It is a journey that requires patience, self-compassion, and a willingness to embrace our imperfections. In a society that constantly bombards us with images of perfection and success, it is easy to fall into the trap of self-doubt and self-criticism. But learning to love and accept ourselves unconditionally is the key to unlocking our full potential and living a truly fulfilling life.

Growing up, I struggled with feelings of inadequacy and self-doubt. As a child, I was always comparing myself to others and felt like I never quite measured up. It wasn't until I began immersing myself in the study of spiritual sciences that I started to understand the importance of self-love. I realized that in order to thrive in this world, I needed to cultivate a deep sense of self-worth.

The journey to self-love is not an easy one. It requires us to confront our fears and insecurities head-on, to look deep within ourselves and acknowledge our past mistakes and shortcomings. But it is through this process of self-reflection and self-awareness that we can begin to heal and grow.

One of the first steps in cultivating self-love is to let go of the need for external validation. We often look to others to validate our self-worth, seeking their approval and praise. But true self-worth can only be found within ourselves. It is about understanding that we are inherently valuable and deserving of love, regardless of what others may think or say.

To foster self-love, it is important to practice self-compassion. We must learn to treat ourselves with the same kindness and understanding that we would offer to a loved one. This means being gentle with ourselves when we make mistakes, forgiving ourselves for past wrongs, and letting go of the need for perfection.

Self-care is another crucial aspect of cultivating self-love. Taking the time to nurture our physical, mental, and emotional well-being sends a powerful message to ourselves that we are worthy of love and care. This could mean engaging in activities that bring us joy, practicing meditation or mindfulness, or engaging in regular exercise. By prioritizing self-care, we are affirming our own value and showing ourselves that we are deserving of love and attention.

Another powerful practice that can help us cultivate self-love is affirmations. Affirmations are positive statements that we repeat to ourselves to reprogram our subconscious mind. By regularly affirming our own worth and reminding ourselves of our inherent value, we can gradually dissolve the negative self-talk and self-limiting beliefs that may have held us back in the past.

It is important to remember that self-love is not a destination but a lifelong journey. There will be times when we stumble and fall, when self-doubt creeps back in, and when we question our worth. But it is in these moments that we must redouble our efforts and remind ourselves that we are worthy of love and acceptance.

Ultimately, learning to love and accept ourselves unconditionally is a radical act of self-empowerment. It is about reclaiming our own power and recognizing that we have the ability to shape our own destiny. By fostering a deep sense of self-worth, we can embark on a life filled with purpose, joy, and fulfillment.

I invite you to embark on this transformative journey with me. Let us learn to embrace our authentic selves, to love ourselves fiercely and unapologetically. In doing so, we not only create a life that is deeply fulfilling for ourselves but also inspire others to do the same.

Remember, you are deserving of love and acceptance exactly as you are. Embrace your journey of self-love, and let your light shine brightly in the world.

Connecting With Nature

In my quest for enlightenment and personal growth, I have come to recognize the profound influence that nature can have on our well-being. From the gentle rustling of leaves to the majestic beauty of a mountain peak, the natural world holds a wisdom and energy that can be transformative. It is a reminder of our interconnectedness with all living beings, a reminder that we are not separate from the environments we inhabit.

Throughout history, many civilizations have recognized and revered the power of nature. Indigenous cultures around the world have long held sacred the land they call home, recognizing that it holds not only physical resources, but also spiritual guidance. Ancient Mayans, for example, built their pyramids in alignment with celestial bodies, believing that the natural world held immense power and knowledge. The sense of awe and reverence they felt when witnessing a sunrise or a blooming flower is something we can still tap into today.

The scientific community is also beginning to unveil the countless benefits that nature has on our physical and mental well-being. Research has shown that spending time in nature can reduce stress levels, lower blood pressure, and boost the immune system. Walking barefoot on the earth, a practice known as grounding, has been found to reduce inflammation and improve sleep. These findings validate what many of us have intuitively known all along - that nature is our greatest healer.

With this knowledge, I have made it a priority in my life to cultivate a deeper connection with the natural world. I make it a point to spend time outdoors every day, whether it be a stroll through a park, a hike in the mountains, or simply sitting under a tree and listening to the birdsong. I find that when I am in nature, my worries and stressors seem to melt away, replaced by a sense of peace and harmony. It is here that I am reminded of the vastness of the universe, the limitless potential that resides within each and every one of us.

One particular practice that has deepened my connection with nature is the art of forest bathing. Originating in Japan, forest bathing, or Shinrin-yoku, involves immersing oneself in the sights, sounds, and smells of the forest. Scientific research has shown that forest bathing can reduce stress hormones, improve mood, and enhance cognitive function. But beyond the scientific findings, there is a profound spiritual experience that occurs when one allows oneself to be fully present in nature - a sense of unity and connection that transcends words.

In my journey to connect with nature, I have also explored various indigenous healing modalities. One such practice is the Native American sweat lodge ceremony, where individuals gather inside a sacred space and are enveloped in the healing energies of the earth. Through intense heat and the release of toxins, the sweat lodge ceremony is a physical and emotional purification, a way of shedding what no longer serves us and reconnecting with our true essence.

Additionally, I have delved into the wisdom of Ayurveda, an ancient Indian system of medicine that emphasizes the importance of living in harmony with nature. Ayurveda teaches us that we are not separate entities, but rather a microcosm of the macrocosm. By aligning ourselves with the natural rhythms of the earth, incorporating herbs and plants into our daily lives, and practicing self-care rituals that nourish the mind, body, and soul, we can tap into the healing power of nature and find balance in our own lives.

As I reflect on my own journey, I am reminded of the countless ways in which nature has supported and guided me. Whether it be through the vibrant colors of a sunset, the soothing aroma of blooming flowers, or the gentle caress of a breeze, the natural world has always provided solace and inspiration. It is a reminder that, despite the chaos that may surround us, there is a deeper wisdom and harmony that we can tap into.

So, I invite you, dear reader, to join me on this journey of connecting with nature. Take a moment to step outside, to breathe in the fresh air, and to listen to the symphony of life that surrounds us. Allow yourself to be fully present in the beauty and wonder of the natural world, and see how it transforms your own life. Let us cultivate a deeper connection with nature, and in doing so, tap into the healing power that lies within us and all around us.

The Art of Letting Go

For much of my life, I held onto beliefs, relationships, and emotions that no longer served me. I was gripping onto the past, afraid to let go and move forward. It was as if I was holding onto a heavy burden, dragging it along with me wherever I went. The weight of these attachments became overwhelming, holding me back from experiencing true joy, peace, and growth.

But then I realized that holding onto these attachments was hindering my spiritual evolution. I understood that in order to fully embrace my highest potential, I needed to release the old and make space for the new. And so, I began my journey of letting go.

The first step in this process was to identify and acknowledge the attachments that were no longer serving me. I had to confront my fears, insecurities, and limiting beliefs head-on. I delved deep into my psyche, reflecting on past experiences and relationships that were holding me back. It required honesty, vulnerability, and the willingness to face my own shadow.

Once I had identified these attachments, I took the courageous step of consciously releasing them. This required a great deal of self-compassion and forgiveness. I had to remind myself that it was okay to let go, that it did not make me weak or inadequate. On the contrary, it was an act of strength and self-love, a choice to prioritize my own growth and happiness.

To aid me in this process, I turned to various healing modalities and practices that I had acquired over the years. I drew upon the wisdom of energy medicine, utilizing techniques such as tapping and energy clearing to release the energetic imprints of these attachments. I also practiced meditation, finding solace and clarity in the stillness of my mind.

Furthermore, I explored the power of breathwork in releasing attachments and embracing the present moment. Through conscious breathing techniques, I was able to let go of old patterns, fears, and attachments that were no longer serving me. Each breath became a symbol of surrender and renewal, a reminder that I was in control of my own journey.

But perhaps the most powerful aspect of this process was the support and guidance of my loved ones. My soulmate, who has been by my side since our teenage years, offered a steady hand and a patient ear. She, too, embarked on her own journey of letting go, allowing us to grow together and create a space for love, growth, and happiness.

As I gradually released these attachments, I began to witness the profound impact it had on my well-being. I felt lighter, freer, and more aligned with my true self. I embraced new perspectives, opportunities, and relationships that were in alignment with my highest purpose. The energy that was once consumed by attachments was now redirected towards my personal growth, creativity, and joy.

But the art of letting go is an ongoing process, a continuous dance with the ebb and flow of life. It requires constant self-awareness, reflection, and the willingness to surrender to the Divine order. It is not always easy, and there are moments of resistance and discomfort. Yet, in those moments, I remind myself of the immense freedom and liberation that come from embracing the art of letting go.

My journey of letting go has taught me that true happiness lies in detachment. By releasing attachments, we create space for growth, love, and abundance to flow into our lives. We invite opportunities and experiences that are in alignment with our highest purpose. We become the creators of our own destiny, free from the shackles of the past.

So, I encourage you, dear reader, to embark on your own journey of letting go. Explore the attachments that no longer serve your growth and happiness. Embrace the discomfort and uncertainty that may arise. Trust in the process and have faith that the universe is guiding you towards your highest good.

Remember, the art of letting go is not about denying or suppressing our emotions and experiences. It is about acknowledging, releasing, and surrendering to the flow of life. It is about choosing growth, happiness, and freedom over stagnation and limitation.

Releasing attachments is a powerful act of self-love and empowerment. It is an invitation to live life fully, embracing the present moment and creating a future that is in alignment with our truest selves. So, let go, my friend, and watch as the magic unfolds.

CHAPTER 3

THE MIND'S JOURNEY

Understanding Consciousness

As I delved deeper into my spiritual journey, I began to explore the limitless realm of consciousness. The more I read and studied, the more I realized that consciousness is not just an abstract concept but a fundamental element that shapes our perception of reality.

My curiosity led me to numerous researchers and studies that sought to unravel the mysteries of consciousness. One such study examined the effects of meditation on the brain and concluded that it can increase neural connections and alter brain structure. This finding suggested that our conscious thoughts and actions have the power to shape our own brains.

Further exploration into the works of neuroscientist David Eagleman revealed the concept of "neuroplasticity," which suggests that our brains have the ability to change throughout our lives. This meant that we could modify our thought patterns, beliefs, and perceptions to create a more empowered and fulfilling existence.

The study of consciousness also led me to the realm of quantum physics, where I discovered the intriguing phenomenon of the observer effect. This principle states that the mere act of observation influences the behavior of subatomic particles. It made me ponder how our consciousness, our thoughts and intentions, could exert a similar influence on our everyday reality.

Drawing from my knowledge of NLP (Neuro-Linguistic Programming), I understood that our perception of reality is shaped by our beliefs, values, and past experiences. Our minds create a subjective representation of the world, filtering and distorting information to fit our preconceived notions. This realization opened my eyes to the fact that there is no objective reality; rather, our perceptions create our individual reality.

To better understand the nature of consciousness, I delved into the works of philosopher René Descartes. He famously stated, "Cogito, ergo sum" – I think, therefore I am. Descartes pointed out that the very act of thinking is proof of our existence. This concept resonated deeply with me, as it implied that consciousness is the essence of our being.

As I began to grasp the significance of consciousness in shaping our reality, I embarked on a personal journey to expand my own awareness. I meditated regularly, allowing my mind to delve into a state of stillness and silence. In those moments of quiet contemplation, I experienced glimpses of pure consciousness beyond the noise and chatter of everyday life.

Beyond meditation, I explored various breathwork techniques that aimed to enhance consciousness. Breathing exercises, such as those I learned from the Science of Life & Breath course and the Dopamine Activated Breathing (DAB) course, helped me access deeper states of awareness and tap into the inherent wisdom of my being.

One of the most profound experiences of investigating consciousness came from practicing the Wim Hof breathing technique. This powerful technique involved controlled hyperventilation followed by breath retention, resulting in heightened states of consciousness and an increased sense of well-being. Through this practice, I began to witness the intimate connection between my breath and my consciousness.

As I continued to delve deeper into the mysteries of consciousness, I realized that it's true nature cannot be fully comprehended through words or intellectual understanding alone. It is a realm that needs to be experienced firsthand, through direct perception and inner exploration.

Understanding consciousness is not just an intellectual pursuit; it is a personal journey that requires us to go beyond the limitations of our minds and connect with our innermost being. It is a journey that calls us to question and transcend our conditioned beliefs and perceptions.

Through my research and personal experiences, I have come to believe that consciousness is the very fabric of existence. It is the invisible force that gives rise to all that we perceive. By understanding consciousness and its role in shaping our perception of reality, we have the power to transform our lives and create a more profound sense of purpose and fulfillment.

In the following chapters of this book, I will share various tools and techniques that have helped me in my own exploration of consciousness. From mindfulness practices to the power of intention, each chapter will delve deeper into empowering ourselves and taking responsibility for our well-being on all levels of existence – physical, mental, emotional, and spiritual.

As I continue my quest as a work in progress, I invite you to join me on this journey of self-discovery and awakening. Together, let us delve into the realm of consciousness, unravel its mysteries, and empower ourselves to live life to its fullest potential.

The Power of Mindfulness

The origins of mindfulness can be traced back to ancient Eastern practices, such as Buddhism and Taoism. These traditions recognized the importance of being fully present in the moment, as a way to cultivate inner peace and clarity. In recent years, mindfulness has gained widespread recognition in the Western world, thanks in large part to the pioneering work of Jon Kabat-Zinn, a professor of medicine and renowned mindfulness teacher.

When I first started exploring mindfulness, it was as if I had stumbled upon a hidden treasure. I had always been an inquisitive soul, searching for answers to life's deeper questions. But it wasn't until I discovered mindfulness that I truly began to understand the power of the present moment. It was like a veil had been lifted, revealing a world of infinite possibilities.

Learning how to cultivate mindfulness is a journey in itself. It requires patience, practice, and a willingness to let go of preconceived notions about the nature of reality. One of the first steps I took on this path was to establish a daily meditation practice. Sitting in stillness, with my eyes closed, I allowed my awareness to settle on the breath. As thoughts arose, as they inevitably do, I learned to observe them without judgment, and gently return my focus to the breath.

In addition to formal meditation, I discovered that mindfulness can be woven into every aspect of daily life. Whether it's eating a meal, taking a walk in nature, or engaging in conversation with a loved one, mindfulness can be applied to enhance our experience. By bringing a nonjudgmental awareness to our senses, thoughts, and emotions, we can fully immerse ourselves in the present moment, without being carried away by the stories of the past or the worries of the future.

Over time, I began to notice subtle shifts in my perception and way of being. I became more attuned to the beauty of the world around me, to the interconnectedness of all things. A profound sense of gratitude began to well up within me, as I realized the preciousness of each passing moment. With each breath, I found myself becoming more grounded, more centered, as if my roots were growing deeper into the earth.

Research has shown that mindfulness can have a wide range of benefits, both for the mind and body. Studies have found that regular mindfulness practice can reduce stress, improve concentration, and enhance overall well-being. It can also help reduce symptoms of anxiety and depression, and even boost our immune system. By training our minds to be more present, we have the power to shape our thoughts, emotions, and ultimately, our lives.

One of the greatest gifts that mindfulness has given me is the ability to cultivate a sense of inner peace amidst the chaos of daily life. It has taught me to be more compassionate towards myself and others, to let go of judgment and embrace acceptance. Through mindfulness, I have come to understand that happiness is not a destination to be reached, but rather a state of being that can be cultivated in the here and now.

In my work as a certified life coach and energy medicine practitioner, I have witnessed the transformative power of mindfulness in the lives of my clients. By helping them develop a mindfulness practice, I have seen them overcome limiting beliefs, heal emotional wounds, and embark on a journey of self-discovery and growth. It is truly remarkable what can happen when we approach life with a beginner's mind, with a sense of curiosity and openness.

As I reflect on my own journey with mindfulness, I am filled with a deep sense of gratitude. It is a practice that has brought me closer to my true self, allowing me to tap into a wellspring of inner wisdom and guidance. Through mindfulness, I have learned that true liberation lies not in changing the external circumstances of our lives, but in cultivating a deep sense of presence and acceptance within ourselves.

I invite you to explore the various techniques and practices that I have found helpful in my own life, and to adapt them to suit your own unique path.

Unraveling Cognitive Processes

What is it that makes us think, learn, remember, and make decisions? How does our mind process information and create meaning out of the world around us? These are questions that have driven me to explore the vast realm of cognitive processes, and the deeper I delve, the more awe-inspiring the answers become.

To explore the intricate processes of cognition is to embark on a journey into the very essence of human existence. It is a journey that requires open-mindedness, curiosity, and a willingness to challenge our preconceived notions of reality. For behind the veil of our conscious thoughts lies a world of subconscious patterns, biases, and mechanisms that shape our perception of the world.

One of the most fascinating aspects of cognitive processes is the role that perception plays in shaping our reality. Our minds are constantly filtering and interpreting the influx of sensory information that bombards us every moment of our waking lives. It is through perception that we construct our reality, creating a unique and personalized version of the world that is influenced by our beliefs, experiences, and cultural conditioning.

But perception is not a passive process. It is a dynamic interplay between our sensory input and our cognitive filters, which include our attention, memory, and emotions. These filters determine what information we pay attention to, what we remember, and how we interpret the world. They are the key to understanding our thought patterns, biases, and beliefs.

To gain insights into how our mind works, we must first understand the power of attention. Our attention is like a spotlight, focusing our awareness on specific aspects of our environment while filtering out the rest. It is through attention that we select what information to process and what to discard, shaping our perception of the world. But our attention is limited, and we can only focus on a fraction of the stimuli that surround us at any given moment.

Memory also plays a crucial role in our cognitive processes. It is through memory that we encode, store, and retrieve information, allowing us to learn from the past and plan for the future. But memory is not a perfect recording of events. It is a dynamic and malleable process that is influenced by our emotions, expectations, and cognitive biases. Our memories are not objective representations of reality, but rather subjective reconstructions that are shaped by our unique perspective.

Emotions, too, are a fundamental aspect of cognition. They color our perception of the world, influencing our thoughts, decisions, and behaviors. They are a direct link between our mind and body, shaping our physiological responses and guiding our actions. Understanding the role of emotions in cognition is key to unlocking the true potential of our mind, as emotions can both empower and hinder our ability to think critically and make rational decisions.

As I delve deeper into my exploration of cognitive processes, I am struck by the interconnectedness of the mind and body. Our thoughts, emotions, and physical sensations are all intertwined, each influencing the other in a delicate dance of feedback loops. To truly understand our cognitive processes, we must embrace a holistic approach that considers the mind, body, and spirit as interconnected systems.

This journey into the intricate processes of cognition has taught me that our minds are powerful tools, capable of both enriching our lives and limiting our potential. By unraveling the mechanisms that underlie our thoughts, emotions, and behaviors, we gain the power to transform our lives and reach new heights of self-awareness and personal growth. It is a journey that requires courage, persistence, and a deep commitment to self-discovery.

So, I invite you, dear reader, to join me on this journey of unraveling cognitive processes. Let us explore the depths of our minds, question our assumptions, and challenge the limitations that hold us back. Together, we can gain insights into how our minds work and empower ourselves to live life to its fullest.

The Influence of Beliefs

Our beliefs are formed throughout our lives, starting from a very young age. They are a culmination of our personal experiences, cultural upbringing, and societal conditioning. These beliefs become deeply ingrained in our subconscious mind and often go unquestioned. We may not even be aware of the beliefs that are shaping our thoughts, emotions, and actions.

For example, growing up, I was conditioned to believe that success was directly correlated with academic achievements and a high-paying job. This belief became the driving force behind my pursuit of a prestigious degree in Electronics Engineering and later, an MBA in Finance. While these accomplishments brought me a certain level of success and recognition in the corporate world, I soon realized that true fulfillment and happiness were not solely dependent on these external achievements.

Through my journey of self-discovery and exploration of spiritual sciences, I began to question the beliefs that shaped my perspective on success and happiness. I started to challenge the notion that material wealth and societal status were the only markers of a fulfilling life. This new perspective opened doors to a realm of infinite possibilities and allowed me to align my actions with my true passions and purpose.

Beliefs not only influence our thoughts but also shape our emotions. If we believe that we are unworthy of love and happiness, we will constantly feel a sense of inadequacy and insecurity. These limiting beliefs create a self-perpetuating cycle of negative thoughts and emotions, which further reinforce the belief.

I experienced this firsthand when I found myself constantly seeking validation and approval from others. I had internalized the belief that my worthiness was dependent on external validation. This led to a constant state of anxiety and a deep-seated fear of rejection. It took years of self-reflection and inner work to challenge and dismantle this limiting belief.

One powerful tool that I utilized in my journey of self-discovery was the practice of affirmations. Affirmations are positive statements that help rewire our subconscious mind by replacing negative beliefs with empowering ones. By consciously repeating affirmations such as "I am worthy of love and happiness," I gradually began to shift my internal dialogue and beliefs about myself. Over time, I noticed a significant improvement in my self-esteem and an increased sense of self-worth.

Another effective strategy to challenge limiting beliefs is through visualization and imagination. Our minds have the incredible ability to create vivid mental pictures of desired outcomes. By visualizing ourselves achieving our goals, we can create new neural pathways and beliefs that align with our aspirations.

For instance, I had always dreamed of becoming a published author, but I held a deep-seated belief that I was not a good writer. This limiting belief prevented me from even attempting to write a book for years. Through visualization exercises and creative visualization techniques, I began to imagine myself as a successful author, receiving praise and recognition for my work. As I visualized this desired reality, I gradually discarded the limiting belief that I was not a good writer. This shift in my beliefs propelled me to take action, and eventually, I published my first book.

Challenging limiting beliefs requires courage, self-reflection, and a willingness to step outside our comfort zones. It is a process of shedding old belief systems that no longer serve us and embracing new beliefs that align with our true desires and potentials.

I encourage you, dear reader, to take a deep dive into your beliefs and question whether they are empowering or limiting. Identify the beliefs that no longer serve you and be willing to replace them with new, empowering beliefs. Remember, you have the power to shape your own reality and create a life that is aligned with your highest potential.

Stay tuned as we delve deeper into the intricate web of thoughts, emotions, and actions that shape our daily lives. The journey towards self-empowerment continues, and we are just scratching the surface of what is possible.

The Role of Perception

Growing up, I always had a curious mind. I questioned everything, wanting to understand the deeper meaning behind the events and circumstances that unfolded before me. This innate curiosity led me on a journey of exploration, not only in the external world but also within myself. I soon realized that perception played a crucial role in shaping my reality.

Our perception is shaped by a myriad of factors, including our upbringing, beliefs, experiences, and culture. It creates a lens through which we view and interpret the world. This lens can either limit us or empower us, depending on how open and flexible it is. If we hold onto rigid beliefs and preconceived notions, our perception becomes narrow and constricted, limiting our ability to see alternative perspectives and opportunities.

However, if we develop a mindset of curiosity and open-mindedness, we can expand our perception, allowing for greater flexibility and adaptability. This enables us to see situations from different angles, think creatively, and make better decisions. Broadening our perspective is about stepping outside of our comfort zone, embracing new ideas, challenging our assumptions, and being willing to consider alternative viewpoints.

One powerful technique for expanding our perception is to practice empathy. Empathy involves putting ourselves in another person's shoes and trying to understand their perspective and emotions. By doing so, we develop a deeper sense of connection and compassion, breaking down barriers and fostering better relationships. In the words of Carl Rogers, "When I accept myself just as I am, then I can change."

Another technique is to engage in mindfulness and present-moment awareness. In the hustle and bustle of daily life, we often get caught up in automatic patterns of thinking and reacting, oblivious to the richness and beauty of the present moment. By practicing mindfulness, we learn to be fully present and in tune with our senses. This allows us to appreciate the small joys of life and cultivate a broader perspective, free from the distractions of the past or worries about the future.

Furthermore, actively seeking out new experiences and exposing ourselves to different cultures, beliefs, and ideologies can profoundly impact our perception. Traveling, reading, attending workshops, or engaging in dialogue with people from diverse backgrounds can open our minds to a world of possibilities, challenging our assumptions and expanding our horizons. By being exposed to different perspectives, we gain a new appreciation for the beauty and wisdom that exist in the diversity of humanity.

In addition to these techniques, I have discovered the profound influence of the subconscious mind on our perception. Our subconscious mind is like a sponge, absorbing information and experiences without our conscious awareness. It stores our beliefs, fears, and desires, shaping our perception and influencing our actions. By delving into the depths of our subconscious mind, we can uncover hidden beliefs and patterns that may be limiting us and reprogram them for a more expansive perception.

Through my journey of self-discovery, I have explored various healing modalities that have aided me in broadening my perspective. As a certified life coach and NLP master practitioner, I have helped clients navigate through limiting beliefs and perceptions, allowing them to embrace their true potential. I have also delved into energy medicine, aromatherapy, and breathwork, all of which have opened portals of insight and transformation. These modalities have not only enhanced my own perception but have offered me the tools to empower others in their own journeys of self-discovery.

In conclusion, perception is a powerful force that shapes our reality. By understanding its role and learning techniques to expand our perspective, we can enrich our lives and embrace the full spectrum of human experience. Through empathy, mindfulness, embracing diversity, and delving into our subconscious mind, we can break free from limited perceptions and open ourselves to new possibilities. The journey of exploration is ongoing, and I invite you to embark on this transformative path of self-discovery. By broadening our perception, we can unlock the true potential that lies within us and live a life of fulfillment and purpose.

The Power of Visualization

Visualization is like a magic wand that we all possess. It is the ability to create vibrant images in our minds, to imagine and see our dreams and goals coming to life. This process harnesses the immense power of our subconscious mind, tapping into its unlimited potential to manifest our desires into reality.

To truly understand the power of visualization, I want to share a fascinating case study that showcases its transformative effects. Meet Radha (Name withheld on request), a young woman who had always dreamt of starting her own fashion brand. She had a deep passion for the art of design and a burning desire to express her creativity. However, like many others, Radha found herself feeling stuck in her current job that offered no fulfillment or satisfaction.

When Radha came to me for guidance, I knew that visualization would be a game-changer for her. We began by setting clear goals, allowing her to envision her dream fashion brand in all its glory. I encouraged her to create a vision board, a collection of images representing her desired outcomes. Each day, she would spend time meditating on her vision board, allowing her mind to fully immerse itself in the world she wanted to create.

As Radha continued to visualize her dream, something remarkable began to happen. She started noticing subtle shifts in her reality. Opportunities began to present themselves, as if the universe was aligning to bring her closer to her goals. She met like-minded individuals who shared her passion for fashion and design, and even stumbled upon a mentor who guided her in taking the necessary steps to turn her dream into a reality. Radha's once stagnant life was now flourishing with possibility and purpose.

Through her journey, Radha discovered the true essence of the power of visualization. It was not merely about daydreaming or wishful thinking, but about aligning her thoughts, emotions, and actions with her desired outcomes. She learned to unlock the dormant potential within herself, unleashing a creative force that propelled her towards her dreams.

But visualization is not just limited to material goals and aspirations. It has the power to positively impact every aspect of our lives, from our relationships to our physical and emotional well-being. It is a tool that can be used to heal, to release limiting beliefs, and to cultivate a deep sense of inner peace and joy.

One powerful technique I often recommend is the use of affirmations during visualization. Affirmations are positive statements that we repeat to ourselves, reinforcing new beliefs and ideas. When combined with visualization, affirmations become amplified, effectively rewiring our subconscious mind to support our desires. For example, if someone is struggling with low self-esteem, they could visualize themselves confidently speaking in public while affirming, "I am confident, capable, and worthy of success."

Another technique that can enhance the power of visualization is the integration of emotions. Emotions are the fuel that drive our intentions and desires, adding potency to the images we create in our minds. By consciously evoking positive emotions such as gratitude, joy, and love while visualizing, we imprint these emotions onto our desired outcomes, magnetizing them towards us.

In my own practice, I have incorporated various visualization techniques that have brought profound changes into my life. One of my favorite techniques is the creation of a mental movie. I vividly imagine myself stepping into a movie theater and watching a movie that represents my desires. I immerse myself in the scene, feeling the emotions, hearing the sounds, and experiencing the sensations as if they were real. This technique has allowed me to cultivate strong belief systems and unwavering faith in my ability to manifest my desires.

Discovering the transformative power of visualization has been a remarkable journey for me. It has opened up a world of infinite possibilities and has empowered me to create the life I truly desire. Through this book, my intention is to provide you with the knowledge and tools to unleash your own creative potential, to manifest your wildest dreams, and to live a life of authenticity, purpose, and fulfillment.

As we delve deeper into the art of visualization, we will explore different techniques, share practical exercises, and delve into the science behind its effectiveness. Together, we will embark on a journey of self-discovery and empowerment, tapping into the boundless power within us to create a life beyond our wildest dreams.

So, my friend, are you ready to step into the realm of visualization and unlock the magic that lies within? Open your mind, open your heart, and let us embark on this transformative adventure together. The power to manifest your desires is within your reach. It is time to awaken the creator within you and embrace the incredible potential that lies beneath the surface. Let us begin.

Nurturing a Growth Mindset

As I embarked on my journey of self-discovery and spiritual awakening, one of the most profound lessons I learned was the importance of nurturing a growth mindset. A growth mindset is the belief that intelligence, abilities, and talents can be developed through dedication, effort, and continuous learning. It is a mindset that allows us to embrace challenges, learn from failures, and unlock our full potential.

Growing up, I was always fascinated by the concept of personal growth and development. I had a thirst for knowledge and a deep desire to understand the mysteries of life. This thirst led me to pursue a diverse range of healing modalities and spiritual practices. Little did I know that these experiences would shape my understanding of the power of a growth mindset.

My journey towards cultivating a growth mindset began with recognizing the limitations of a fixed mindset. A fixed mindset is the belief that our abilities are fixed and cannot be changed. It is a mindset that hinders growth and progress, keeping us trapped in a cycle of self-doubt and fear. I realized that in order to truly unlock my full potential and live a life of purpose and fulfillment, I needed to transcend the confines of a fixed mindset and embrace the limitless possibilities of a growth mindset.

The first step towards cultivating a growth mindset is to embrace challenges. Challenges are not to be feared, but rather embraced as opportunities for growth and self-improvement. I began seeking out challenges in various aspects of my life, whether it was taking on new projects at work, pushing myself physically during my fitness routines, or exploring new avenues of knowledge and learning. By stepping out of my comfort zone and embracing these challenges, I discovered the immense power that lies within me to overcome obstacles and achieve personal growth.

But embracing challenges is just the beginning. Learning from failures is equally important in nurturing a growth mindset. Failure is not a sign of incompetence or inadequacy; it is simply a stepping stone towards success. Each failure holds valuable lessons and insights that can guide us towards improvement and mastery. I learned to view failures as opportunities for growth and reflection, rather than as setbacks. Through each failure, I gained valuable wisdom and experience that propelled me forward on my journey of self-discovery.

Unlocking our full potential requires a commitment to continuous learning. The journey of personal growth is an ongoing process, one that requires us to constantly seek knowledge, expand our horizons, and challenge our existing beliefs and assumptions. I immersed myself in a wide range of spiritual practices, from meditation to energy healing, constantly seeking new ways to expand my understanding of the world and my place in it. I became a certified life coach, energy medicine practitioner, and NLP master practitioner, among other things. These certifications not only enriched my personal growth journey but also equipped me with the tools and knowledge to help others unlock their full potential.

In our society, we often tend to view intelligence and abilities as fixed traits. We label ourselves and others as either "smart" or "not smart," "talented" or "untalented." But this limiting belief only serves to stifle our growth and potential. Cultivating a growth mindset means breaking free from these labels and embracing the idea that abilities can be developed through hard work, dedication, and perseverance.

One of the most powerful ways to nurture a growth mindset is through the power of positive self-talk. Our thoughts have a profound impact on our beliefs and actions. By consciously fostering positive and empowering thoughts, we can rewire our brains to embrace growth and overcome self-limiting beliefs. I started practicing positive affirmations daily, reminding myself of my unlimited potential and the ability to overcome any obstacle that comes my way. This simple practice had a transformative effect on my mindset, allowing me to approach challenges with confidence and resilience.

As I continued on my journey of self-discovery and personal growth, I realized that cultivating a growth mindset is not a one-time event but an ongoing process. It requires consistent effort, self-reflection, and a willingness to step outside of our comfort zones. But the rewards are immeasurable. A growth mindset opens up a world of possibilities, empowering us to embrace challenges, learn from failures, and unlock our full potential.

In conclusion, nurturing a growth mindset is the key to living a life of purpose, fulfillment, and self-empowerment. By embracing challenges, learning from failures, and committing to continuous learning, we can unlock the limitless potential that resides within us. It is a journey of self-discovery and personal growth that requires dedication, perseverance, and a willingness to embrace the unknown. As I continue to evolve on my own path, I am reminded that I am a work in progress, constantly learning and growing, reaching towards my highest potential. And I invite all those who are willing to take responsibility for their well-being on all levels - physical, mental, emotional, and spiritual - to join me on this transformative journey of cultivating a growth mindset and embracing the fullness of life.

Taming the Monkey Mind

In my quest to master this art, I have immersed myself in various healing modalities that have not only transformed my personal life but also provided me with a valuable skill set to assist others on their spiritual journey. Through extensive research, personal experiences, and interactions with spiritual masters, I have unmasked the hidden treasures of quieting the restless mind and cultivating inner peace and clarity.

To embark on this path of self-discovery, one must first recognize the importance of taking responsibility for their well-being on all levels of existence. This includes our physical, mental, emotional, and spiritual realms. Only when we acknowledge the interconnectedness of these aspects of our being can we truly experience a profound sense of peace and clarity.

One of the strategies I have learned in my pursuit of taming the monkey mind is the practice of mindfulness. Mindfulness is the art of being fully present in the moment, without judgment or attachment to our thoughts. By developing this skill, we can gradually detach ourselves from the incessant chatter of the mind and embrace the tranquility that lies within. Through mindfulness, we learn to observe our thoughts without getting entangled in them, allowing us to experience a sense of inner calm amidst the chaos of daily life.

Another powerful technique that has aided me in quieting my restless mind is meditation. Meditation is not just a practice but a lifestyle. It is a dedicated effort to bring stillness to the mind and connect with our inner essence. Through consistent meditation practice, we can train ourselves to detach from our thoughts and become observers of our own minds. This allows us to cultivate clarity, as we begin to recognize patterns, tendencies, and triggers that govern our thought processes. With this heightened awareness, we can consciously choose how to respond to thoughts and emotions that arise within us, rather than being swept away by them.

Breathwork is another vital tool in the journey of taming the monkey mind. By consciously regulating our breath, we can harness the power of our life force energy, or prana, and channel it towards inner peace and clarity. Breathwork exercises such as the Wim Hof Method, Dopamine Activated breathing, and Transcendental Meditation breathwork have been instrumental in helping me achieve a deep sense of tranquility. Through these practices, I have gained an intimate understanding of the profound connection between the breath and the mind, and how they influence one another.

In addition to these practices, I have explored the wisdom of ancient spiritual traditions and integrated them into my personal journey of taming the monkey mind. The teachings of yogic philosophy, for instance, have provided me with valuable insights into the nature of the mind and the importance of self-awareness. By incorporating yogic principles into my daily life, such as practicing non-attachment and cultivating gratitude, I have been able to quieten the restlessness of the mind and embrace a state of inner peace.

Furthermore, I have delved into the scientific research surrounding the mind and its potential for transformation. The field of neuroplasticity has revealed that our brains have the remarkable ability to rewire themselves. By engaging in repetitive, positive practices such as meditation, we can reprogram our neural networks, paving the way for new patterns of thinking and emotional well-being.

Through my own personal experiences and the knowledge I have gathered, I have come to realize that taming the monkey mind is not a destination but an ongoing journey. It requires dedication, patience, and a deep commitment to self-discovery. It is a process of peeling away the layers of conditioning and reconnecting with our true essence.

As I continue to evolve and explore the depths of my own consciousness, I invite others to join me on this incredible journey. Together, we can empower ourselves and cultivate inner peace and clarity, allowing us to truly savor the beauty and richness of life.

In the pages that follow, I will share with you the strategies, techniques, and insights that have revolutionized my own spiritual path. Through the exploration of mindfulness, meditation, breathwork, yogic philosophy, and the marvels of neuroplasticity, we will embark on an adventure that will awaken the dormant potential within each of us. Let us embark on this voyage of self-discovery, for it is through our collective journey that we shall unleash the true power of our minds and transcend the limitations of the mundane.

CHAPTER 4

THE NATURE OF DESIRE

Understanding Desire

To truly understand desire, we must first recognize its multifaceted nature. Desire is not simply a fleeting emotion or a passing thought. It runs much deeper than that. It is the very essence of our being, the driving force behind everything we do. It is the longing within us that seeks fulfillment, that yearns for something more.

But desire is not always as straightforward as it may seem. It is a complex interplay of various factors that shape its manifestation. It is influenced by our past experiences, our environment, and our cultural conditioning. It is molded by our genetic makeup and our individual personalities. And yet, at its core, desire is a fundamental human experience that transcends all these external factors.

One of the most intriguing aspects of desire is its role in shaping our actions and decisions. It is often said that we are creatures of desire, driven to seek out pleasure and avoid pain. And while this may be true to some extent, desire goes much deeper than simple pleasure-seeking.

Desire is an inherent part of our evolutionary journey. It is the driving force that compels us to grow, to learn, and to evolve. It is desire that pushes us beyond our comfort zones, that encourages us to take risks, and that fuels our creative endeavors. Without desire, there would be no progress, no innovation, and no growth.

But desire is not without its pitfalls. The very same force that propels us forward can also lead us astray. It has the potential to cloud our judgment, to blind us from seeing the bigger picture. We can become obsessed with our desires, losing sight of what truly matters in life. We can find ourselves trapped in a never-ending cycle of chasing after external validation, always seeking that next hit of pleasure or success.

To truly understand desire and its role in our lives, we must be willing to examine it with an open mind. We must be willing to question our own motivations and intentions. We must be willing to look beyond the surface and delve deep into the depths of our own being.

One way to gain a deeper understanding of desire is through self-reflection. By taking the time to introspect and examine our own desires, we can begin to unravel the complex web of thoughts, emotions, and conditioning that shape our actions. We can start to differentiate between our genuine desires and those that are imposed upon us by society or by our own insecurities.

Another way to gain insight into desire is through mindfulness. By cultivating a moment-to-moment awareness of our thoughts and emotions, we can develop a greater understanding of the underlying motivations and intentions behind our desires. We can begin to discern whether our desires are aligned with our true values and aspirations, or whether they are driven by external pressures or irrational impulses.

Ultimately, understanding desire is a lifelong journey. It is a process of self-discovery and self-mastery. It requires patience, persistence, and a willingness to confront our own desires with honesty and compassion. It is a journey that takes us beyond the surface level of fleeting pleasures and superficial gratification, and leads us towards a deeper, more meaningful experience of life.

As I reflect upon my own journey of understanding desire, I am reminded of the countless hours spent studying spiritual sciences, exploring different healing modalities, and immersing myself in the wisdom of ancient traditions. Through my various breathing courses, my certifications as a life coach and energy medicine practitioner, and my ongoing pursuit of self-improvement, I have come to realize that desire is not something to be feared or suppressed, but rather something to be understood and embraced.

And so, I invite you, dear reader, to embark upon this journey of self-discovery with me. Let us explore the nature of desire together, and uncover the profound wisdom that lies within. Let us challenge our preconceived notions and expand our understanding of what it truly means to desire. And let us empower ourselves to not only shape our actions and decisions in alignment with our true desires but also to enjoy life to its fullest, on all levels of existence.

For it is through this understanding of desire that we can truly awaken to the infinite potential that resides within us, and embark upon a journey of self-realization and fulfillment.

This is my invitation. Will you accept?

Uncovering True Needs

The first step in uncovering our true needs is to understand the difference between wants and needs. Wants are often driven by external factors such as societal expectations, trends, or the influence of others. They are transient and ever-changing, rooted in the pursuit of material possessions, validation, or success. On the other hand, needs are intrinsic to our being. They are the core elements that contribute to our overall well-being, happiness, and personal growth.

To better understand this distinction, let us imagine a scenario where I am contemplating buying a new car. At first glance, it may seem like a want since it is driven by the desire for something new, stylish, and impressive. However, upon deeper reflection, I realize that my true need is reliable transportation to facilitate my daily activities. The need for a car arises from practical considerations, such as commuting to work, taking my children to school, and running errands. By recognizing this distinction, I can make a conscious decision to align my desires with my true needs.

Aligning desires with true needs requires a process of self-reflection and introspection. It requires us to delve into our innermost thoughts and emotions, to uncover the underlying motives behind our wants and desires. This process can be facilitated by various practices, such as meditation, journaling, or engaging in therapeutic modalities like EFT and NLP. Through these practices, we can gain a deeper understanding of ourselves, our values, and what truly brings us joy and fulfillment.

Once we have identified our true needs, the next step is to align our desires with them. This involves a shift in mindset and a conscious effort to prioritize what truly matters to us. For example, if my true need is to experience a deeper connection with nature, I may realize that my desire for material possessions or career success is not aligned with this need. Instead, I may choose to spend more time in nature, engage in activities that nourish my connection with the natural world, and let go of the external pressures that distract me from my true needs.

Aligning desires with true needs also requires a willingness to let go of attachments and expectations. Often, we hold onto desires that no longer serve us, either out of fear or a sense of obligation. By releasing these attachments, we create space for new possibilities and experiences that are in line with our true needs. This may involve letting go of relationships, careers, or material possessions that no longer align with our growth and well-being. It can be a challenging and uncomfortable process, but it is an essential step towards living a fulfilling and authentic life.

To navigate this journey of aligning desires with true needs, it is essential to cultivate self-awareness, self-compassion, and a sense of purpose. Through regular self-reflection and introspection, we can gain clarity on our true needs and the desires that align with them. We can also develop the inner strength and resilience to let go of limiting beliefs and societal expectations that hinder our growth and fulfillment.

In my own journey, I have discovered the transformative power of aligning desires with true needs. By prioritizing my true needs and letting go of external expectations, I have experienced a profound sense of freedom, fulfillment, and inner peace. I have shifted my focus from the pursuit of material possessions and societal validation to a deeper connection with myself, others, and the world around me.

I invite you to embark on this journey of uncovering your true needs. Take the time to reflect on what truly brings you joy, nourishment, and fulfillment. Let go of attachments and expectations that no longer serve you. Embrace the process of aligning your desires with your true needs, and witness the transformation that unfolds as you embark on a path of self-discovery, empowerment, and a life lived in alignment with your deepest values and aspirations.

In conclusion, I would like to emphasize that this journey is not a one-time event but an ongoing process. As we evolve and grow, our desires and true needs may also shift. Therefore, it is vital to regularly revisit and reassess our priorities, ensuring that our desires remain aligned with our evolving true needs. By doing so, we can continue to experience a sense of fulfillment and joy, living an authentic life in alignment with our true selves.

Overcoming Attachment

As I continued on my journey of self-discovery, one theme kept recurring in my studies: the power of detachment. It was a concept that initially seemed counterintuitive to me. How could letting go of attachments bring us closer to freedom and happiness?

I delved deeper into this topic, immersing myself in various spiritual teachings, psychological frameworks, and personal experiences. What I discovered was life-transforming. The ability to detach from the outcomes of our actions and find contentment in the present moment is a gateway to true liberation.

The concept of detachment can be challenging to grasp, especially in a world that constantly bombards us with messages of achievement and success. We are conditioned to attach our worth to external markers of success, such as wealth, status, and recognition. But as I delved into the spiritual sciences and explored the teachings of enlightened masters, I understood that true fulfillment lies not in the attainment of external goals but in embracing the present moment with an open heart.

Detachment, in its essence, is the ability to let go of the need to control outcomes. It is surrendering to the flow of life and trusting that the universe has a grand plan for us. We often hold tightly to our desires, and when reality doesn't match our expectations, we experience disappointment, frustration, and even despair. But when we learn to detach from these expectations, we open ourselves up to a whole new realm of possibilities.

One of the keys to detach from attachment is cultivating mindfulness. Mindfulness is the practice of being fully present in the moment, without judgment or attachment. It allows us to observe our thoughts, emotions, and sensations without getting entangled in them. Mindfulness brings us back to the here and now, helping us let go of worries about the future or regrets about the past.

As a busy marketing professional and a father of two, finding time for mindfulness practices was initially a challenge. But I realized that even in the midst of a hectic day, I could tune in to the present moment. I started incorporating short meditation breaks into my routine, taking a few minutes to close my eyes, focus on my breath, and bring my full attention to the present. These micro-moments of mindfulness gradually expanded, creating a sense of spaciousness and calm within me.

Another powerful practice that helped me cultivate detachment was journaling. I started writing down my desires, goals, and expectations, and then explored the underlying fears and attachments associated with them. By shining a light on these attachments, I could consciously choose to let go of them, freeing myself from their grip.

It's important to note that detachment does not mean apathy or indifference. It is about embracing life fully while relinquishing our attachment to specific outcomes. We can still set intentions and work towards our goals, but we release the need for things to unfold exactly as we imagine. This shift in mindset allows us to embrace uncertainty, adapt to change, and find joy in the journey itself.

Detachment also involves cultivating a sense of trust and surrender. Trusting in the larger intelligence that governs the universe and surrendering our personal will to the divine can be challenging, especially for those of us accustomed to taking control. But as I learned to surrender, I realized that there is a greater plan at play, and sometimes the path to our highest good unfolds in ways we could never have anticipated.

Through my exploration of detachment, I also discovered the profound connection between detachment and gratitude. When we let go of attachments and embrace the present moment, we open ourselves up to a deep appreciation for life's blessings. Gratitude becomes a natural response, and we find ourselves noticing and savoring the beauty and abundance that surround us.

Practicing detachment requires ongoing self-awareness and self-compassion. We all have attachments and desires that can pull us back into the cycle of grasping. However, with practice, we can gently observe these attachments and choose to release them, moment by moment. It is a journey, not a destination, and there will be times when we stumble or fall back into old patterns. But the key is to always come back to the present moment, reminding ourselves of the freedom and joy that lie in letting go.

In conclusion, detachment is not an easy path, but it is a path that leads to profound inner freedom. By learning to detach from attachment to outcomes and finding freedom in the present moment, we open ourselves up to a life of greater fulfillment, peace, and joy. Through mindfulness, journaling, trust, surrender, and gratitude, we can cultivate detachment and transform our relationship with life. It is my hope that this exploration of detachment will empower you to embark on your own journey of self-discovery and awaken to the beauty and infinite possibilities that exist within and around you.

The Illusion of Pleasure

In our society, pleasure is often equated with happiness. We are conditioned to seek immediate gratification, pursuing pleasure in various forms - be it through material possessions, indulging in rich food, seeking sensual experiences, or even achieving fame and success. We chase after these fleeting moments of pleasure, convinced that they will bring us lasting joy. But as I delved deeper into this illusion, I discovered a truth that shook me to my core.

Pleasure is merely a temporary sensation, a fleeting high that fades away as quickly as it arrives. It is like a mirage in the desert, alluring from afar but vanishing upon closer inspection. I began to question the impermanence of pleasure and its ability to truly sustain us. Was there something more beyond this illusion?

My quest for answers led me down a path of self-exploration and spiritual awakening. I realized that lasting fulfillment cannot be found in external sources alone. It lies deep within us, waiting to be awakened and nurtured. The key to unlocking this inner fulfillment was to examine the transient nature of pleasure and explore alternative sources of lasting joy.

As I delved into my research, I came across various studies and teachings that supported my newfound understanding. Neuroscientists have discovered that pleasure is produced in our brain through the release of dopamine, a neurotransmitter associated with reward and pleasure. However, this pleasure response diminishes with repeated exposure to the same stimulus, leading to a phenomenon known as habituation. In simple terms, the more we seek pleasure, the less pleasure we derive from it.

This revelation shook me to the core, making me question the very fabric of our society. We are bombarded with messages that promise instant gratification, and we believe that accumulating more pleasure will lead to happiness. But in reality, it could be the very pursuit of pleasure that deprives us of true fulfillment.

So, where do we find lasting joy? How do we break free from the cycle of seeking pleasure in external sources that inevitably leave us unsatisfied? The answer lies within us, in the realm of our inner being and spiritual essence.

In my own pursuit of lasting fulfillment, I have explored various spiritual practices and healing modalities. Whether it be energy medicine, aromatherapy, or breathwork, each modality has enabled me to delve deeper into my own being, connecting with the essence of who I truly am. It is through these practices that I have come to realize the innate wisdom and strength that reside within, waiting to be awakened.

But the journey to lasting fulfillment is not a linear path. It requires effort and dedication to break free from the allure of temporary pleasure and embrace a higher purpose. It is about acknowledging that true joy comes from within, not from the external world. It is about cultivating gratitude, living in the present moment, and aligning our actions with our deepest values.

As I look back on my own experiences, I am humbled by the transformative power of this journey. It has taught me to cherish the simple pleasures of life - a warm embrace, a shared laugh, or the beauty of nature. It has shown me that lasting fulfillment resides not in the accumulation of material possessions, but in the relationships we nurture, the love we give and receive, and the purpose we find within ourselves.

Dear reader, I invite you to embark on this journey of self-discovery with me. Let us shed the illusion of pleasure and explore the deeper sources of lasting fulfillment. Let us free ourselves from the chains of immediate gratification and embrace the wisdom that lies within us. Together, we can empower ourselves and take responsibility for our well-being on all levels of existence - physical, mental, emotional, and spiritual.

Are you ready to awaken to the truth of lasting fulfillment? Join me as we dive into the depths of our souls and emerge with a renewed sense of purpose, joy, and connection. The time has come for us to break free from the illusion of pleasure and embrace the ecstasy of our own awakening.

Cultivating Contentment

In our fast-paced and ever-changing world, it is not uncommon to find ourselves constantly seeking more. More money, more success, more possessions, more validation from others. We are conditioned to believe that true happiness lies in the attainment of external factors, leading us to constantly strive for bigger and better things. However, in this never-ending pursuit, we often forget to simply be present and appreciate the joy that can be found in the present moment.

I have always been fascinated by the concept of contentment. How is it that some individuals seem to radiate a genuine sense of peace and satisfaction, regardless of their external circumstances? What is their secret? These questions have led me on a personal journey to discover the art of contentment and the role it plays in our overall well-being.

My exploration into the world of contentment began with a deep dive into the realm of spiritual sciences. Through my studies, I came to understand that true contentment stems from an inner state of being, rather than the acquisition of external possessions or achievements. It is about finding joy in the present moment, no matter what our circumstances may be.

One of the first steps I took towards cultivating contentment was to develop a daily gratitude practice. I realized that by consciously focusing on the blessings in my life, big and small, I could shift my perspective and cultivate a sense of appreciation for what I already had. Each morning, I would take a few moments to reflect on the things I was grateful for – the love of my family, the beauty of nature, the opportunities life had bestowed upon me. This simple practice enriched my life and allowed me to find joy in the simplest moments.

Another powerful tool in my journey towards contentment was the practice of mindfulness. Mindfulness is about being fully present in the here and now, without judgment or attachment to the past or future. Through mindfulness, I was able to let go of unnecessary worries and anxieties that were stealing my peace of mind. I learned to savor the tastes, sights, and sounds of each moment, recognizing that true happiness is found in the present, not in the pursuit of future desires.

A key aspect of cultivating contentment is learning to let go of the need for external validation. Our society often measures success based on external markers such as wealth, status, and achievements. However, true contentment comes from within and cannot be gained through the approval or validation of others. I had to learn to detach myself from societal expectations and focus on my own inner journey. This meant embracing my true passions and values, regardless of whether they aligned with societal norms or not. I discovered that when we live in alignment with our authentic selves, true contentment naturally follows.

In my quest for contentment, I also delved into the field of positive psychology. This branch of psychology focuses on understanding the factors that contribute to human flourishing and well-being. It emphasizes the importance of cultivating positive emotions, such as gratitude, hope, and joy, in order to lead fulfilling lives. Drawing from this knowledge, I began to incorporate simple practices into my daily routine that would boost my overall sense of well-being. These included engaging in activities that brought me joy, nurturing positive relationships, practicing self-care, and setting realistic goals that were in alignment with my values.

Over time, I realized that contentment is not a destination to be reached, but rather a way of living. It requires a shift in mindset and a conscious choice to find joy in each moment. It is about choosing to focus on what we have, rather than what we lack. It is about accepting the present moment, with all its imperfections, and finding peace within ourselves.

In conclusion, cultivating contentment is an art that requires practice and conscious effort. It is a journey of self-discovery and inner growth. By incorporating practices such as gratitude, mindfulness, self-acceptance, and positive psychology, we can learn to find joy in the present moment and experience true contentment. It is my hope that this book will serve as a guide for all those who are willing to embark on this journey of self-empowerment and find fulfillment in their lives.

The Role of Gratitude

Throughout my spiritual journey, I have come to realize that the role of gratitude is of utmost importance. It is not merely a fleeting emotion or a polite gesture of saying thank you; it is a way of life. Gratitude is the key that unlocks the door to true happiness and fulfillment.

In our busy lives, it is easy to take things for granted and get caught up in the whirlwind of negativity and stress. We often focus on what is lacking rather than what we already have. However, cultivating a grateful mindset can shift our perspective and allow us to see the goodness that exists in every moment.

One of the most powerful lessons I have learned is that gratitude is a choice. We have the ability to choose how we perceive our reality and what we focus our attention on. When we consciously choose to cultivate gratitude, we create a positive feedback loop in our lives. The more we express gratitude, the more blessings and abundance we attract.

To explore the transformative power of gratitude, it is important to understand its many benefits. Research has shown that practicing gratitude on a regular basis can lead to improved physical and mental well-being. It has been linked to lower levels of stress and depression, increased feelings of happiness and contentment, and improved relationships.

Gratitude has a profound impact on our health and well-being. When we are grateful, our bodies release hormones and neurotransmitters that promote relaxation, reduce inflammation, and boost our immunity. This not only improves our physical health but also enhances our ability to cope with challenges and bounce back from adversity.

On a mental and emotional level, gratitude has the power to rewire our brains and shift our mindset from scarcity to abundance. It allows us to focus on the positive aspects of our lives, no matter how small or insignificant they may seem. By directing our attention towards what we are grateful for, we train our brains to find joy and positivity in every situation.

One of the most effective practices to cultivate a grateful mindset is keeping a gratitude journal. Each day, take a few moments to write down three things you are grateful for. It could be something as simple as a warm cup of tea in the morning, a hug from a loved one, or a beautiful sunset. By consistently focusing on the blessings in your life, you will start to notice a shift in your overall outlook and attitude.

Another powerful practice is expressing gratitude towards others. Take the time to thank the people in your life who have made a difference, whether it is with a handwritten note, a heartfelt conversation, or a simple smile. When we acknowledge and appreciate the contributions of others, we not only strengthen our relationships but also create a ripple effect of gratitude in the world.

Gratitude is not limited to external circumstances; it encompasses our own self-appreciation as well. Take the time to honor and celebrate your own accomplishments, no matter how small they may seem. Give yourself permission to acknowledge the growth and progress you have made on your journey. By cultivating self-gratitude, you boost your self-esteem and create a positive foundation for further growth and learning.

In addition to these practices, there are various techniques and rituals that can deepen your experience of gratitude. Meditation, for instance, allows you to quiet your mind and connect with the present moment. By focusing on your breath and repeating gratitude affirmations, you can cultivate a deep sense of appreciation for the here and now.

Nature can also be a powerful catalyst for gratitude. Spend time in the great outdoors, connecting with the beauty and wonder of the natural world. Whether you take a walk in the park, hike in the mountains, or simply sit by the ocean, allow yourself to be fully present and in awe of the miracles that surround you.

The transformative power of gratitude is not limited to our personal lives; it extends to our relationships, work, and the world at large. When we approach each interaction and situation with a grateful mindset, we create a ripple effect of positivity and kindness. We become agents of change, spreading love and gratitude wherever we go.

As I reflect on my own journey with gratitude, I am humbled by the immense blessings that have come into my life. From the loving relationship I share with my soulmate and the joyous moments with my children, to the opportunities for growth and learning in my career, gratitude has been the guiding force that has allowed me to fully embrace and appreciate the richness of life.

I invite you to explore the transformative power of gratitude in your own life. Embrace the practice of cultivating a grateful mindset and witness the magic unfold. By expressing gratitude for every moment, every person, and every experience, you will find yourself living a life of joy, abundance, and deep fulfillment.

Remember, gratitude is a choice. Choose gratitude, and let it awaken the true essence of your being.

Balancing Desires and Needs

Desires are the manifestations of our innermost dreams, the things that set our soul on fire and drive us towards greater achievements. They come from a place of passion, ambition, and a longing for expansion and growth. Our desires fuel our motivation and serve as a beacon guiding us towards a future defined by our deepest aspirations.

On the other hand, needs are the fundamental elements required for our overall well-being and nourishment. They encompass our physical, mental, emotional, and spiritual needs, all of which need to be acknowledged and addressed for us to experience true fulfillment. Neglecting our needs can lead to a state of imbalance, where our desires become overshadowed by feelings of dissatisfaction, unhappiness, and a lack of fulfillment.

So how do we find the balance between pursuing our desires and meeting our true needs for holistic fulfillment? It calls for a deep introspection and an understanding of our own unique desires and needs. It is essential to distinguish between the external influences that shape our desires and the internal yearnings that define our needs. This awareness helps us make conscious choices, ensuring that our actions align with our authentic selves.

The first step is to identify our desires with clarity. What do we truly want? Often, our desires are influenced by societal expectations, the media, or the desires of those around us. It is important to peel away these external layers and tap into our own inner wisdom. Only then can we understand what truly lights up our soul and ignites our passion.

Once we are clear about our desires, we can then turn our attention to our needs. These needs are the pillars that support our overall well-being. They include the physical aspects such as nutrition, exercise, and rest; the mental aspects such as learning, personal growth, and intellectual stimulation; the emotional aspects such as love, connection, and self-expression; and the spiritual aspects such as purpose, meaning, and connection to something greater than ourselves.

Finding the balance between desires and needs requires prioritization and conscious decision-making. It may mean making sacrifices or reevaluating our definition of success. It is about understanding that true fulfillment comes from aligning our desires with our needs and creating harmony between the two.

I have come to realize that the pursuit of desires without addressing our needs can lead to a life of endless seeking. We might achieve external success, but if our needs are neglected, we will always feel a sense of emptiness deep within us. Similarly, focusing solely on meeting our needs without considering our desires can lead to a life devoid of passion and purpose.

To find this balance, we must nurture ourselves on both the physical and the metaphysical planes. It requires us to take care of our bodies, minds, hearts, and souls. It asks us to pay attention to what truly nourishes us and aligns with our deepest values and aspirations.

Through my own spiritual journey, I have discovered various practices that help in balancing desires and needs. Breathwork, meditation, and mindfulness have allowed me to tap into my intuition and connect with my true desires and needs. These practices have helped me cultivate self-awareness, allowing me to make conscious choices in alignment with my authentic self.

Moreover, the study of energy healing modalities has further enriched my understanding of the interconnectedness of our desires and needs. By working with subtle energies, I have learned that our desires can be aligned with our needs, creating a harmonious flow of energy within us. When we are in such a state of balance, our desires become vehicles for our personal growth and evolution.

It is important to note that the balance between desires and needs is not a static state but an ongoing process of self-discovery and self-care. As we evolve and grow, our desires and needs may also change. It is through this continuous exploration that we can find the sweet spot where our desires fuel our growth, our needs nurture our well-being, and our lives become a true expression of our authentic selves.

In conclusion, finding the balance between pursuing our desires and meeting our true needs for holistic fulfillment is a lifelong journey. It requires self-reflection, self-awareness, and conscious decision-making. By aligning our desires with our needs, we can create a life of purpose, passion, and true fulfillment. It is through this delicate dance that we awaken the power within and embark on a path of self-empowerment and self-mastery.

Aligning Actions With Aspirations

For years, I too found myself caught in this cycle of externally imposed goals and aspirations. As a marketing professional in a travel retail organization, I was successful by society's standards. My degrees in Electronics Engineering and Finance had opened doors for me, and my career was flourishing. But despite the external trappings of success, I felt a nagging emptiness deep within me. There was a yearning for something more, something meaningful that was not defined by material possessions or societal accolades.

That yearning led me on a journey of self-discovery and spiritual exploration. I delved into the world of spiritual sciences, seeking answers to the questions that haunted me. I attended workshops, took courses, and became certified in various healing modalities. But while these teachings provided me with valuable insights, it wasn't until I embraced a holistic approach to well-being that I truly began to align my actions with my aspirations.

I soon realized that aligning my actions with my deepest values and aspirations was not simply a conceptual exercise but required practical strategies and daily commitment. It demanded a conscious effort to live my life in alignment with my true essence, to make choices that honored my values, and to be mindful of the impact of my actions on myself and others.

One of the key strategies I adopted was the practice of mindfulness. I began to cultivate present moment awareness, paying attention to my thoughts, emotions, and actions. Through this practice, I developed a deeper understanding of myself and the patterns that were holding me back from living in alignment with my aspirations. I discovered that many of my actions were driven by fear, societal expectations, and a need for external validation. Mindfulness allowed me to recognize these patterns and make conscious choices that were in alignment with my true values.

Another strategy that brought me closer to aligning actions with aspirations was the practice of setting clear intentions. I began to ask myself, "What do I truly want in life?" Instead of focusing solely on external achievements, I started to explore my deepest desires and aspirations. I discovered that my true values lay in connection, growth, and service. Armed with this clarity, I set intentions that reflected these values in every aspect of my life - from my career to my relationships.

But setting intentions alone was not enough. It required a commitment to take action and make conscious choices every day. To facilitate this process, I created a daily routine that supported my aspirations. I incorporated practices such as meditation, journaling, and physical exercise into my day to cultivate a sense of inner balance and alignment. These practices not only helped me connect with my highest self but also provided me with the clarity and focus needed to take aligned action.

As I delved deeper into my journey, I also discovered the power of self-reflection and self-inquiry. I regularly took time to assess my actions and their alignment with my aspirations. I asked myself questions such as, "Am I living in integrity with my values?" and "Are my actions bringing me closer to my deepest desires?" This self-inquiry became a potent tool for self-awareness and course correction, allowing me to realign my actions whenever they veered off track.

Throughout this process, I learned that aligning actions with aspirations is not a one-time achievement but an ongoing practice. It requires constant self-awareness, reflection, and adjustment. It demands a willingness to let go of old patterns, beliefs, and ideas that no longer serve us. It requires us to step outside of societal expectations and forge our own path, guided by our unique values and aspirations.

Today, as I look back on my journey, I am grateful for the wisdom and growth that aligning actions with aspirations has brought into my life. I am no longer defined by societal standards of success but by my own sense of purpose and fulfillment. I have come to understand that true alignment comes from within, from honoring our deepest values and desires, and from living a life that is authentic and true to ourselves.

My hope is that by sharing my experiences and the strategies that have helped me on this path, I can inspire and empower others to align their actions with their deepest values and aspirations. We are each on our own unique journey, but through conscious choices and a commitment to self-discovery, we can all find our own path of alignment and live a life that is rich and meaningful. It is never too late to awaken to our true selves and step into the fullest expression of who we are. The choice is ours.

CHAPTER 5

OBJECTIFYING THE WORLD

Subject and Object

To truly comprehend the concept of subject and object, one must first understand that these terms are not confined to philosophical or spiritual discussions alone. They are pervasive in every aspect of our existence, determining how we perceive the world around us and how we interact with it.

At its core, the concept of subject refers to the self, the individual consciousness that is the observer, the experiencer. It is the "I" that perceives, thinks, feels, and acts. On the other hand, the object is everything that is perceived, whether it be the external world, events, people, or even our own thoughts and emotions. The object is everything that is outside of the self, the "other" in relation to the subject.

However, it is important to recognize that the subject and object are not independent entities but are deeply intertwined, constantly influencing and shaping each other. The way we perceive the world and the events happening around us is profoundly colored by our subjective experiences, beliefs, and conditioning. In turn, our perceptions and interpretations of the world influence our thoughts, emotions, and actions, creating a continuous feedback loop.

To fully grasp the significance of this interplay, let's consider a simple example. Imagine standing in front of a beautiful sunset, where the subject is your consciousness, and the object is the majestic display of colors painted across the sky. In this scenario, your perception of the sunset is not solely based on the physical attributes of the scene but is heavily influenced by your subjective experiences, emotions, and beliefs.

For instance, if you were going through a period of sadness, you might perceive the sunset as melancholic, as though it reflects your internal state. Conversely, if you were in a state of joy and contentment, the same sunset might fill you with a sense of awe and wonder, reinforcing your positive emotions.

This simple example highlights how our subjectivity shapes our reality, how our internal state colors our perception and interpretation of the external world. It shows that our experiences are not simply a result of what happens around us but are deeply influenced by our inner landscape.

However, it is crucial to recognize that while we are active participants in shaping our reality, we are not entirely in control of it. We cannot control the external events or the actions of others, but we can choose how we respond to them. This power lies within our ability to shift our perspective, to transform our subjectivity, and thereby alter our experience of the world.

In my spiritual journey, I have come to understand that this transformation begins with self-awareness, with becoming conscious of our conditioned patterns of thinking, feeling, and behaving. By observing our subjective experience, we can gain insight into the beliefs, fears, and limitations that color our perception of the world.

Through practices such as meditation, mindfulness, and introspection, we can develop a deep awareness of our subjective lens, allowing us to question and challenge our conditioned patterns. This process of self-inquiry helps us cultivate a more expansive and fluid perception, allowing for growth and transformation.

As I continue on my own path of self-discovery, I have realized the immense power of the subject-object interplay in shaping not only our individual realities but also our collective experience. By recognizing our role as active participants in co-creating our reality, we can begin to take responsibility for our well-being on all levels of existence.

This recognition empowers us to shift our focus from the external to the internal, from seeking happiness and fulfillment in the outside world to cultivating it within ourselves. It invites us to explore the depths of our being, to embrace our innate wisdom and inherent divinity.

Through this exploration, we discover that our true nature transcends the duality of subject and object. We realize that we are not separate from the world around us but intimately interconnected with it. We recognize that our actions have ripple effects that extend far beyond our individual lives, shaping the collective consciousness and influencing the world we inhabit.

As we awaken to this profound understanding, we realize the potential for transformation and healing. We realize that by nourishing our own well-being and embodying love, compassion, and authenticity, we can contribute to the evolution of our collective consciousness.

In conclusion, the concept of subject and object invites us to explore the interplay between our subjective experiences and the external world, between our perception and the reality we create. It reminds us that our experiences are not fixed or predetermined but are malleable, shaped by our consciousness.

By embracing this understanding and committing to our own growth, we can transcend the limitations of our conditioned patterns and open ourselves to the infinite possibilities that exist within and around us. We can become conscious creators of our reality, empowered to live a life that is aligned with our deepest truths and highest potential.

I invite you, dear reader, to embark on this profound journey of self-discovery and empowerment. Let us explore together the limitless depths of our being, discovering the magic that unfolds when we tap into our true essence. May this awakening be the catalyst for your own transformation, as we journey hand in hand towards a reality that is more vibrant, joyful, and harmonious.

The Power of Perspective

To truly understand the power of perspective, let us delve deeper into its definition and context. Perspective, in its simplest form, refers to a particular point of view or way of seeing things. It is a subjective lens that is shaped by our beliefs, experiences, values, and biases. Our perspective is unique to us, influencing our thoughts, emotions, and actions.

In a world of infinite possibilities, it is crucial to recognize that there is never just one fixed perspective. Every situation offers multiple angles, each carrying its own truth. However, our inherent human tendency is to cling to a singular perspective, often unaware of the limitations it imposes on our growth and understanding.

By harnessing the power of perspective, we can broaden our horizons, challenge our assumptions, and unlock new possibilities. It allows us to step beyond the confines of our comfort zone and embrace the vastness of the unknown. Through a shift in perspective, we gain the ability to reframe challenges into opportunities, turn obstacles into stepping stones, and find beauty in the most mundane aspects of life.

Discovering the transformative power of perspective requires a conscious effort and a willingness to embrace change. The first step is to cultivate self-awareness, which involves a deep exploration of our own beliefs, values, and biases. It is through this introspective journey that we begin to unravel the layers of conditioning and societal expectations that have shaped our perspective.

Once we have gained a clear understanding of our current perspective, we can then explore techniques to shift our point of view. One such technique is reframing, which involves consciously choosing to see a situation from a different angle. It allows us to break free from unhelpful patterns of thinking and open ourselves up to new interpretations and possibilities.

In addition to reframing, mindfulness is another powerful tool that can aid in shifting our perspective. By practicing mindfulness, we develop the ability to observe our thoughts, emotions, and sensations without judgment. This non-judgmental awareness helps us see situations more objectively, liberating us from the limitations of our preconceived notions.

The power of perspective can also be harnessed through empathy, the ability to step into another person's shoes and see the world through their eyes. Empathy expands our consciousness and fosters compassion, allowing us to develop a deeper understanding of others and their perspectives. It breaks down barriers, cultivates connection, and paves the way for personal and societal transformation.

Furthermore, seeking diverse perspectives and engaging in meaningful dialogue with people of different backgrounds and beliefs can also broaden our understanding. By actively listening and valuing others' viewpoints, we enrich our own perception of reality and create space for growth and learning.

As I reflect upon my own journey, I realize that the power of perspective has played a pivotal role in my personal and spiritual growth. Through my exploration of various healing modalities and spiritual practices, I have come to appreciate the interconnectedness of all aspects of existence. I have learned to embrace the ebb and flow of life, to find peace within chaos, and to see beauty in the simplest of moments.

My travels have exposed me to diverse cultures, each with its own unique perspective on life. From the vibrant streets of Mumbai to the tranquil mountains of the Himalayas, I have witnessed the richness that lies in embracing different ways of living and thinking. I have had the privilege of engaging in deep conversations with fellow seekers who have challenged and expanded my perspective, pushing me to question my beliefs and explore the uncharted territories of my consciousness.

In my quest for deeper understanding, I have immersed myself in various breathing techniques and practices that have allowed me to tap into the power of the present moment. The rhythmic beat of my tabla and the melodic strumming of the guitar have offered me a transcendent experience, enabling me to connect with the pulse of the universe. Nature has been my sanctuary, a constant reminder of the interconnectedness of all beings and the importance of harmonizing our perspective with the natural world.

As I continue on my journey, I am acutely aware that my perspective is ever-evolving. I am a student, forever learning and unlearning, eager to embrace the infinite possibilities that lie ahead. The power of perspective has taught me that we are not limited by our circumstances, but by the limitations we impose upon ourselves. It has empowered me to take responsibility for my own well-being on all levels – physical, mental, emotional, and spiritual – and to live life to its fullest.

Through this book, I invite you, dear reader, to embark on your own journey of self-discovery and transformation. I urge you to question your perspective, challenge your beliefs, and explore new ways of seeing the world. By embracing the power of perspective, you can unlock the full potential of your being and pave the way for a life of joy, fulfillment, and deep connection. So, let us embark on this enlightening journey together and embrace the awakening that awaits us.

Embracing Multiple Realities

I had always believed in the power of perception and the subjective nature of reality. But I had never truly considered the idea that different individuals could experience completely different versions of the world. It was a profound realization that shattered the boundaries of my consciousness. I began to question everything I knew and sought to expand my understanding.

My exploration began with extensive reading and research on quantum physics and consciousness. I discovered the groundbreaking theories of physicists like Max Planck, Erwin Schrödinger, and Niels Bohr, who proposed that reality is a product of perception and observation. Their work suggested that there are multiple potential realities that exist simultaneously, waiting to be collapsed into a single experience through conscious observation.

This notion resonated deeply with me, and I embarked on a journey to explore the depths of this concept. I attended workshops and seminars, engaging with renowned experts in the field. I learned about the power of intention and manifestation, understanding that our thoughts and beliefs shape the reality we experience.

One particular workshop focused on the art of lucid dreaming—an ability to become conscious within the dream state. Lucid dreaming allowed individuals to navigate alternate realities, gaining insights and experiences that were impossible within the confines of the physical world. As I delved into this practice, I unearthed profound wisdom and self-discovery, learning to expand my consciousness beyond the limitations of my waking life.

I also sought wisdom from ancient spiritual traditions that held similar beliefs about the existence of multiple realities. The concept of parallel universes, for example, was prevalent in Hinduism and Buddhism, where it was believed that there were countless realms and dimensions coexisting with our own. I immersed myself in these teachings, finding solace and inspiration in their ancient wisdom.

With a newfound understanding of multiple realities, I started embracing diverse perspectives in my daily life. I began to recognize that every person carries a unique lens through which they perceive the world. Each perspective is shaped by a multitude of factors—culture, upbringing, education, and personal experiences. It was a humbling realization that allowed me to approach conversations and interactions with an open heart and mind.

Embracing diverse perspectives meant actively seeking out different viewpoints and listening without judgment. I engaged in conversations with people from different backgrounds and walks of life, curious to understand their perceptions and lived experiences. Stepping into their reality, even for a brief moment, widened my own perspective and enriched my understanding of the world.

I also discovered the power of empathy in embracing multiple realities. By putting myself in someone else's shoes, I could feel their joys, sorrows, and struggles. Empathy allowed me to connect deeply with others and build bridges of understanding. It dissolved the boundaries that separated us, revealing the interconnectedness of all beings and the shared human experience.

As I continued my exploration, I realized that embracing multiple realities was not just an intellectual exercise, but a transformative spiritual practice. It required me to let go of my ego, my preconceived notions, and the need to be right. It demanded humility and an unwavering commitment to personal growth.

Through this journey, I learned to discern between what I believed to be true and what others believed. I understood that my truth was subjective, and so was everyone else's. Instead of clinging to a single perspective, I began to embrace a tapestry of diverse beliefs and experiences, understanding that they all contributed to the rich fabric of existence.

Embracing multiple realities also meant accepting the existence of paradoxes and contradictions. I discovered that life was not about finding absolute truths but navigating the ever-changing nuances of existence. It required me to be comfortable with uncertainty and surrender to the mysteries of the universe.

In conclusion, the journey of embracing multiple realities has been transformative and enlightening. It has allowed me to break free from the limitations of a singular perspective and embrace the boundless possibilities of the human experience. By exploring diverse perspectives, questioning my own beliefs, and seeking wisdom from various sources, I have come to understand that the richness of life lies in the tapestry of multiple realities. It is a journey that continues to unfold, and I am grateful for the lessons it has taught me.

The Role of Bias

As human beings, we are naturally prone to biases. Biases are mental shortcuts that help us process information quickly by relying on preconceived notions and stereotypes. They can be both conscious and unconscious, affecting our thoughts, beliefs, and behavior. Our biases are shaped by a multitude of factors, including our upbringing, culture, education, and personal experiences. They color our perception, often leading us to make judgments and decisions that may be distorted or unfair.

One common bias that many of us experience is confirmation bias. Confirmation bias is the tendency to seek out and interpret information in a way that confirms our pre-existing beliefs. We are more likely to accept information that aligns with our worldview and reject or ignore information that challenges it. This bias can limit our ability to consider alternative perspectives and hinder our personal growth.

Another bias that influences our perception is the halo effect. The halo effect occurs when we form a general impression of a person based on a single characteristic or trait. For example, if we find someone physically attractive, we may automatically assume that they possess other positive qualities as well. This bias can lead us to overlook flaws or make inaccurate judgments about others.

Understanding these biases is crucial because they have a pervasive impact on various aspects of our lives, including our relationships, decision-making, and self-perception. However, just as biases can cloud our perception, they also offer us an opportunity for growth and self-awareness. By becoming aware of our biases and actively working to overcome them, we can cultivate a more objective and empathetic perspective.

So how can we overcome our biases? One strategy is to practice mindfulness and self-reflection. Engaging in regular introspection allows us to become more aware of our thoughts and beliefs, enabling us to identify any biases that may be influencing our perception. By questioning our assumptions and seeking out diverse perspectives, we can actively challenge and broaden our understanding of the world.

Another strategy is to cultivate empathy. Empathy is the ability to understand and share the feelings of another person. By developing empathy, we can strive to see the world through the eyes of others, allowing us to transcend our biases and cultivate compassion and understanding. This can be achieved through active listening, seeking out diverse voices and experiences, and engaging in meaningful conversations.

Education also plays a vital role in overcoming biases. By exposing ourselves to diverse perspectives and learning about different cultures, beliefs, and experiences, we can challenge our own biases and develop a more nuanced understanding of the world. Education empowers us to question our assumptions and biases, fostering a more inclusive and tolerant society.

In addition to these strategies, it is crucial to approach information with a critical mindset. In an age where we are bombarded with information from various sources, it is essential to be discerning consumers of information. Fact-checking, seeking out multiple sources, and being open to revising our beliefs based on new evidence are all essential practices in overcoming our biases.

Overcoming biases is not an easy task. It requires self-awareness, humility, and a commitment to lifelong learning. It requires us to confront our own limitations and actively engage in self-reflection. However, the rewards are immense. By striving to overcome biases, we can develop a more objective and compassionate perspective, fostering a world that is more inclusive and tolerant.

As I continue on my own spiritual journey, I am reminded of the importance of examining and challenging my biases. It is a continuous process, one that requires dedication and self-awareness. But with each step I take towards overcoming my biases, I find myself growing closer to my true self and connecting with others on a deeper level.

In this chapter, we have explored the influence of biases on our perception and the strategies we can employ to overcome them. And as we delve further into the depths of self-exploration, let us remember that our perception shapes our reality, and by cultivating a more objective and empathetic perspective, we can truly awaken to the beauty and potential that lies within us and the world around us.

Expanding Consciousness

To truly expand our consciousness, we must first open ourselves up to the idea that there is more to life than what meets the eye. We must acknowledge that there is a vast and interconnected web of energy that permeates every aspect of our existence. And then, we must have the courage to explore this unseen realm, to venture into the depths of our own consciousness and, ultimately, to embrace the interconnectedness of all things in the universe.

I believe that the key to expanding our consciousness lies in developing a sense of awe and reverence for the mysteries of the universe. It is through this sense of wonderment that we can begin to perceive the interconnectedness of all things. When we allow ourselves to be fully present in the moment, when we open our hearts and minds to the beauty and complexity of the world around us, we begin to see the threads that connect us to everything else.

One of the most powerful tools that I have discovered in my journey of expanding consciousness is meditation. Through the practice of meditation, we can quiet the incessant chatter of our minds and tap into a deeper, more expansive state of awareness. In this state, we can begin to perceive the subtle energies that flow through us and connect us to the greater whole. We can experience a sense of unity and interconnectedness with all living beings, with nature, and with the entire cosmos.

In addition to meditation, I have also explored various healing modalities to expand my consciousness. These modalities, such as energy medicine and breathwork, have allowed me to tap into the power of my own energetic field and to connect with the universal energy that surrounds us. Through these practices, I have witnessed profound shifts in my own health and wellbeing, as well as in the lives of those around me.

Research has shown that expanding consciousness has a direct impact on our mental and emotional wellbeing. Studies conducted by neuroscientists have shown that regular meditation practice can lead to changes in brain structure, increasing the size of certain regions associated with emotional regulation and compassion. This suggests that expanding our consciousness not only allows us to connect with others on a deeper level, but also helps us to cultivate a greater sense of empathy and understanding.

Expanding our consciousness also has a ripple effect on our physical health. Research has shown that meditation and other mindfulness practices can reduce stress, lower blood pressure, and boost the immune system. By cultivating a state of heightened awareness and presence, we can tap into the body's innate ability to heal itself and maintain optimal health.

But expanding consciousness is not just about personal growth and self-improvement. It is a collective journey, one that has the power to transform society as a whole. As more and more individuals awaken to the interconnectedness of all things, we can begin to shift our perspective from one of separation and division to one of unity and collaboration. This shift in consciousness has the potential to create profound and lasting change in our world, as we come together to address the pressing issues that face humanity and the planet.

In conclusion, expanding consciousness is a deeply transformative journey that opens us up to the interconnectedness of all things in the universe. Through practices such as meditation, energy healing, and mindfulness, we can tap into the power of our own consciousness and connect with the greater whole. By expanding our awareness, we can cultivate a greater sense of empathy, compassion, and unity, both within ourselves and in relation to others. This journey is not just a personal one, but a collective one, with the potential to create a more conscious and harmonious world for all beings.

The Power of Empathy

In my journey of self-discovery and spiritual exploration, I have come to recognize the immense importance of empathy in building meaningful relationships and fostering true connection. It is not a mere act of kindness, but rather a conscious choice to be present and truly listen to another person's story without judgment or agenda.

Cultivating empathy has been an ongoing process for me, requiring a deep commitment to self-reflection and a willingness to look beyond the surface. It is about embracing vulnerability, letting go of our own preconceived notions, and embracing the power of human connection.

One of the most profound experiences that taught me the power of empathy was when I attended a workshop on Compassionate Communication. The workshop was led by a renowned spiritual teacher who taught us that true empathy starts with understanding our own emotions and needs. By acknowledging and accepting our own inner experiences, we become better equipped to understand and connect with others on a deeper level.

During the workshop, we were asked to partner up and share an experience in our lives that had brought us pain or suffering. As I listened to my partner recount her story of loss and heartbreak, I found myself being deeply touched by her vulnerability and honesty. In that moment, I realized the immense power of simply being present and holding space for another person's emotions. It was not about offering advice or fixing their problems; it was about cultivating a genuine connection based on love and understanding.

Empathy is not limited to personal relationships; it is a powerful tool that can be harnessed in professional settings as well. As a marketing professional, I have witnessed firsthand the impact of empathy in the workplace. By taking the time to truly understand the needs and desires of our customers, we can create marketing campaigns that resonate on a deeper level. By empathizing with our colleagues and co-workers, we can foster a work environment that is supportive, collaborative, and inclusive.

In today's fast-paced world, where technology has made communication instantaneous but often shallow, empathy is more crucial than ever. It is that human touch that reminds us of our shared humanity, that we are all interconnected and deserving of compassion. It is a reminder that we are not alone in our struggles and that by reaching out and extending empathy, we can create a ripple effect of kindness and understanding.

To cultivate empathy, we must be willing to embrace vulnerability and step out of our comfort zones. It requires a deep level of self-awareness and a willingness to challenge our own biases and assumptions. It is about actively listening to others, not just with our ears, but with our hearts. It is about being present and fully engaged, setting aside distractions and truly investing our time and energy into connecting with others.

Through my own spiritual journey, I have learned that empathy is not something that can be taught or learned overnight. It is a lifelong practice, a choice that we must make each day. It is about being open to the experiences of others, even when they seem foreign or unfamiliar. It is about celebrating our differences and recognizing the universal human emotions that bind us all together.

As I continue to explore the depths of my own spiritual awakening, I am constantly reminded of the power of empathy. It is a guiding principle that shapes my interactions with others and allows me to forge deeper, more meaningful connections. It is a practice that has taught me to look beyond the surface and embrace the beauty of shared human experiences.

In conclusion, cultivating empathy is not just a way to connect with others; it is a path to self-discovery and personal growth. By extending empathy to those around us, we create a ripple effect of love and understanding that has the power to transform not only our relationships but also the world around us. So, let us dare to be empathetic, to step into the shoes of others and truly understand their joys, sorrows, and struggles. Let us choose empathy, for it is through empathy that we can truly awaken to the interconnectedness of all beings and the power of love and compassion.

Embodying Compassion

But what does it truly mean to embody compassion? It goes beyond superficial gestures of sympathy or pity. Embodying compassion means cultivating a deep sense of empathy within ourselves, allowing us to truly understand and connect with the experiences and emotions of others. It means being present for someone, offering a listening ear, and creating a safe and non-judgmental space for them to express themselves. It means being willing to make ourselves vulnerable and open to others, even when it may be uncomfortable or challenging.

In our fast-paced and often self-centered world, it is easy to overlook the importance of compassion. We have become so wrapped up in our own lives and concerns that we forget to consider the struggles and joys of those around us. We become blind to the pain and suffering of others and fail to recognize that we are all interconnected, all part of a larger web of existence. Embodying compassion is a constant reminder of this interconnectedness, urging us to recognize our shared humanity and to treat one another with kindness and respect.

I have witnessed the transformative power of compassion in my own life and in the lives of others. When we approach situations with empathy and understanding, we create a ripple effect of positivity and healing. Compassion has the ability to dissolve the barriers of separation, to bridge the gaps between individuals, communities, and nations. It is the antidote to division, prejudice, and hatred, and it holds the key to fostering a world of peace and harmony.

So how do we learn to embody compassion? It begins with self-compassion. We must first learn to be kind and understanding towards ourselves, acknowledging our own flaws, mistakes, and vulnerabilities without judgment. This practice of self-compassion allows us to cultivate a wellspring of compassion within our own hearts, enabling us to extend it outward to others.

I have explored various healing modalities in my quest for spiritual growth, and they have all taught me valuable lessons about compassion. Energy medicine, life coaching, and breathwork have shown me that compassion starts with attuning to the present moment, to the needs and feelings of those we encounter. It requires us to set aside our own ego and desires, and to truly listen and connect with others on a deep and meaningful level.

As we learn to embody compassion, we become agents of change in the world. We become beacons of light, igniting the potential for healing and transformation in others. It is not always an easy path to walk, for there will be challenges and moments of doubt along the way. But when we choose compassion, we choose love over fear, unity over division, and kindness over cruelty.

In a world that often seems chaotic and divisive, embodying compassion becomes an act of rebellion. It is a radical choice to see humanity in others, to extend empathy and understanding even when it may not be reciprocated. It is an invitation to create a society that is rooted in compassion, where no one is left behind or marginalized. It is a call to action, urging us to actively seek out opportunities to practice compassion in our daily lives.

I invite you, dear reader, to join me on this journey of embodying compassion. Let us learn to see the world through the lens of empathy and understanding. Let us extend kindness and love to all beings, regardless of their backgrounds or circumstances. As we cultivate compassion within ourselves, we create a ripple effect that touches the lives of many. Together, let us co-create a world where compassion is not just a concept, but a lived experience for all.

Embracing Unity in Diversity

Growing up in India, a country known for its cultural diversity, I was exposed to different religions, languages, traditions, and beliefs from a very young age. It was a melting pot of cultures, where people from various backgrounds coexisted harmoniously. This vibrant tapestry of diversity ignited a curiosity within me, urging me to explore the foundations of unity that lay at the core of this diversity.

My journey began by seeking out knowledge in various spiritual sciences. I devoured books and attended workshops and seminars, each one revealing a new layer of understanding about the interconnectedness of all existence. It was this quest for knowledge that led me to become a certified life coach, energy medicine practitioner, aromatherapist, and NLP master practitioner. Each modality provided me with a different lens through which to view the world and comprehend the unity that lay beneath the surface.

I soon realized that embracing unity in diversity was not just a philosophical concept, but a way of life. It required us to celebrate the beauty of diversity by appreciating the unique gifts and perspectives that each individual brings to the table. Only by recognizing and valuing these differences can we truly harness the power of unity.

In India, festivals like Diwali, Eid, Christmas, and Holi serve as beautiful reminders of the unity that exists within our diverse society. These celebrations bring people from different religious and cultural backgrounds together, creating an atmosphere of love, joy, and inclusivity. The colors, aromas, and melodies of these festivals fill the air with a sense of unity, reminding us that despite our differences, we are all part of the same human family.

But unity in diversity is not confined to geographical boundaries. It transcends borders and embraces the entire world. Through my travels, I have had the opportunity to witness the power of unity in action. Whether it is in the bustling markets of Marrakech, the serene temples of Bali, or the vibrant streets of New York City, the underlying unity is palpable. It is in the shared laughter and the warmth of human connections that we find the true essence of unity.

At a deeper level, embracing unity in diversity requires us to explore the interplay of the physical, mental, emotional, and spiritual aspects of our existence. It calls upon us to recognize the unity that exists within ourselves and to embrace all aspects of our being, both light and shadow. Only by accepting and integrating these different facets can we truly experience unity in its entirety.

To delve deeper into this exploration, I have undertaken various breathing courses and practices. The Science of Life & Breath, Dopamine Activated Breathing, and Transcendental Meditation Breathwork have all opened doors to new levels of self-awareness and connection. These practices have taught me that the breath is not just a physiological process, but a bridge between the physical and spiritual realms. It is through the breath that we tap into the universal life force energy that flows within and around us, enhancing our sense of unity with all of existence.

As a fitness enthusiast, I have also found that physical activity and being in nature greatly contribute to cultivating a sense of unity. Whether it is going for a run in the park, a hike in the mountains, or practicing yoga on the beach, these activities allow me to connect with the natural world and its inherent unity. The rhythm of my feet hitting the ground, the wind rustling through the trees, and the sun kissing my skin all remind me of the interconnectedness of all living beings.

As I continue to explore unity in diversity, I am constantly reminded of the importance of self-reflection and personal growth. It is only through inner transformation that we can truly embody the principles of unity and empathy. This journey is ongoing, and I affectionately refer to myself as a work in progress. Each day brings new lessons, new challenges, and new realizations that further fuel my passion for exploring unity in all its magnificent forms.

In this book, I hope to share my experiences, insights, and wisdom with all those who are willing to embark on their own journey of self-discovery and empowerment. It is my belief that by embracing unity in diversity, we can create a world where love, compassion, and understanding are the guiding principles. This unity has the power to transcend all boundaries and heal the divisions that exist within our global community.

So let us celebrate the beauty of diversity and explore the unity that underlies all existence. Let us learn from one another, embrace our differences, and cultivate an unwavering sense of unity in our daily lives. Together, we can create a world where everyone is valued and respected for who they are, and where the power of unity prevails in every facet of our being.

CHAPTER 6

THE PATH TO FULFILLMENT AND ENLIGHTENMENT

Uncovering Your Life's Purpose

Throughout my own personal journey, I have discovered various techniques and practices that have helped me uncover my life's purpose. These methods are not one-size-fits-all; they are a compilation of different tools that have resonated with me. I encourage you to explore and experiment with them, allowing your intuition to guide you towards what feels right for you.

The first technique I want to share is self-reflection. This practice involves setting aside dedicated time to introspect and delve into the depths of our being. Find a quiet space where you can be alone, free from distractions.

Take a few deep breaths, grounding yourself in the present moment. Close your eyes and ask yourself, "What is my purpose in life?" Allow the question to permeate your being, and be open to whatever answers arise.

Another approach that has been instrumental in my own journey is journaling. Writing allows us to tap into our subconscious mind and access deeper layers of our being. Set aside regular time each day to write freely, without judgment or censorship. Let your thoughts flow onto the paper, exploring your dreams, passions, and values. Reflect on past experiences that have brought you joy and fulfillment. Notice any patterns or recurring themes that emerge. Journaling helps to clarify our thoughts, illuminating our true passions and desires.

Meditation is a powerful tool that can bring us closer to our life purpose. By quieting the mind and fully immersing ourselves in the present moment, we create space to access our inner wisdom. Find a comfortable seated position, close your eyes, and focus on your breath. As thoughts arise, observe them without attachment, allowing them to pass by like clouds in the sky. As you become more centered and grounded, ask yourself, "What is my purpose?" Be open to any insights or inspirations that arise during your meditation practice.

In addition to these introspective practices, I have found that seeking guidance from mentors and spiritual teachers can greatly assist in uncovering our life's purpose. Engage in conversations with individuals who have already embarked on their own purposeful journey. Seek out their wisdom and guidance, asking for their insights and experiences. These mentors can offer fresh perspectives, helping us gain clarity and inspiration on our own path.

It is important to remember that uncovering our life's purpose is not a linear or straightforward process. It requires patience, self-compassion, and a commitment to self-exploration. Embrace each step of the journey, even the moments of uncertainty and doubt, knowing that they are all part of the process. Trust that your purpose will reveal itself in divine timing, and continue to take inspired action towards aligning your life with your soul's calling.

As you begin to uncover your life's purpose, it is essential to align your actions with it. Take intentional steps towards manifesting your purpose, integrating it into all areas of your life. Identify the activities and projects that align with your passions and values, and commit to pursuing them wholeheartedly. This may require letting go of old patterns and beliefs that no longer serve you, and embracing new ways of being and doing. Remember that alignment with your purpose is not a one-time task; it requires continuous self-awareness and adjustment as you grow and evolve.

Throughout my own journey, I have discovered that living in alignment with my purpose has brought a sense of fulfillment and joy that is unparalleled. I have witnessed the profound impact it has had on my relationships, my work, and my overall well-being. It has allowed me to step into my authentic self, fully embracing who I am and what I have to offer to the world.

I invite you to embark on this transformative journey of uncovering your life's purpose. Embrace the uncertainty, the challenges, and the moments of profound clarity. Trust in your inner wisdom and guidance, and know that you have a unique purpose that is waiting to be expressed. Remember, you are a work in progress, and this exploration of purpose is an ongoing process. Embrace the journey, and may it lead you to a life of meaning, fulfillment, and divine purpose.

Following Your Passion

What if I told you that the key to unlocking your true potential lies in following your passion? What if I told you that by pursuing what truly lights you up, you can tap into a transformative power that will not only change your life but also the lives of those around you? Imagine a world where everyone is living their lives with purpose and fulfillment, where happiness and success abound. This is the world that awaits those who have the courage to follow their passion and embark on a journey of self-discovery and personal growth.

My Journey of Passion:

For as long as I can remember, I have always been drawn to the mystical unknown, to the exploration of spiritual sciences. My career in marketing may have provided stability and financial security, but it was my passion for the study of spiritual sciences that truly ignited my soul. It was a calling that I could no longer ignore.

I had always been a seeker, hungry for knowledge and eager to uncover the deeper truths of life. My educational background in engineering and finance had equipped me with valuable skills, but they were merely stepping stones on my path towards self-realization. My thirst for spiritual knowledge led me to pursue various healing modalities and gain certifications in life coaching, energy medicine, aromatherapy, and Neuro-Linguistic Programming (NLP). Each step was a revelation, deepening my understanding of the interconnectedness of the physical, mental, emotional, and spiritual aspects of our being.

Discovering the Transformative Power:

It was during my journey of exploring different breathing techniques that I truly discovered the transformative power of following my passion. The Science of Life & Breath course offered by the Pratibimb charitable trust shed light on the importance of conscious breathing in maintaining physical and mental well-being. Through practices such as Dopamine Activated Breathing (DAB) and Transcendental Meditation breathwork, I experienced profound healing and a heightened sense of awareness. The breath became my gateway to unlocking the vast potential within me.

As I delved deeper into the world of breathwork, I came across the Wim Hof method, an active breathwork technique renowned for its ability to boost energy levels, improve focus, and enhance overall health and well-being. Learning and practicing this technique not only invigorated my physical body but also strengthened my connection to my inner self. It was through the power of conscious breathing that I truly began to understand the essence of following my passion.

Pursuing What Truly Lights You Up:

Following your passion is not merely about finding a hobby or indulging in something you enjoy in your leisure time. It goes beyond that. Pursuing what truly lights you up means aligning your life with your core values, beliefs, and interests. It means stepping into your authentic self and embracing the unique gifts and talents that have been bestowed upon you. It is a path of self-discovery, growth, and fulfillment.

When you pursue your passion, you tap into a reservoir of inner strength and resilience. Challenges become stepping stones rather than obstacles. Failures become opportunities for growth and learning. Life becomes a canvas on which you can create your masterpiece.

Not only does following your passion lead to personal fulfillment, but it also has a ripple effect on those around you. When you are passionate about what you do, your energy, enthusiasm, and zest for life are contagious. You inspire others to embrace their own passions and embark on their own journeys of self-discovery. You become a catalyst for positive change, not only in your own life but in the lives of others as well.

Living Life to Its Fullest:

In a world where we are constantly bombarded with societal expectations, peer pressure, and the fear of judgment, it takes courage to follow your passion. It takes courage to break free from the shackles of conformity and embrace your true self. But when you do, the rewards are immeasurable.

By following your passion, you are no longer merely existing; you are truly living life to its fullest. You experience a sense of joy, purpose, and fulfillment that transcends material possessions and external achievements. You become the best version of yourself and inspire others to do the same.

So, I urge you, dear reader, to take a moment and reflect on what truly lights you up. What makes your heart sing and your soul dance with joy? What brings you a sense of purpose and fulfillment? Embrace your passion, no matter how unconventional or insignificant it may seem to others. For it is through the pursuit of what truly lights you up that you will discover the transformative power that lies within you. It is through following your passion that you will unlock your true potential and create a life of purpose, joy, and fulfillment.

Cultivating Inner Peace

As I delved deeper into my spiritual journey, I realized that cultivating inner peace was not a destination but a continuous journey, a way of life. In the chaotic hustle and bustle of daily life, finding serenity seemed like an elusive quest. However, I discovered that with consistent practice and dedication, it was possible to create an oasis of inner peace amidst the chaos.

Step 1: Embracing Mindfulness

Mindfulness became the foundation of my quest for inner peace. It involved staying present in the moment, fully aware of my thoughts, emotions, and physical sensations. It meant letting go of regrets from the past and worries about the future. By cultivating mindfulness, I learned to observe my inner experiences without judgment, creating a space for peace to flourish.

One of the techniques I found particularly helpful was conscious breathing. Taking a few moments each day to focus on my breath allowed me to anchor myself in the present moment, clearing my mind of the clutter and noise that often consumed me. Through conscious breathing, I discovered that inner peace was not an external state to be achieved, but rather an intrinsic aspect of my being.

Step 2: Practicing Gratitude

Gratitude became my secret weapon in the pursuit of inner peace. It was easy to get caught up in the negativity and stress of daily life, but by consciously cultivating gratitude, I shifted my focus towards the abundance and beauty that surrounded me. Each morning, I started my day by writing down three things I was grateful for. It could be as simple as the warmth of the sun or the smile of a loved one. This small practice instilled a profound sense of peace and contentment within me.

Step 3: Nurturing Self-Compassion

In the midst of our hectic lives, it is easy to become our harshest critic. We beat ourselves up for our mistakes and shortcomings, often neglecting the importance of self-compassion. I realized that inner peace could only be sustained if I treated myself with kindness and understanding.

To nurture self-compassion, I began practicing self-care. This meant prioritizing activities that brought me joy and nourished my soul. Whether it was taking a leisurely walk in nature, savoring a cup of tea, or simply curling up with a good book, I made it a point to carve out time for myself each day. By honoring my needs and desires, I discovered that I became more centered, allowing inner peace to radiate from within.

Step 4: Connecting with Nature

Nature has a way of soothing our souls and bringing us back to a state of peace and harmony. I made it a priority to spend time in nature, whether it was going for a hike in the mountains, walking barefoot on the beach, or simply basking in the beauty of a blooming flower. The sights, sounds, and scents of nature had a profound effect on my well-being, grounding me and reminding me of the inherent peace that exists within all of us.

Step 5: Cultivating Loving-Kindness

As I ventured further along my spiritual path, I realized the interconnectedness of all beings. Cultivating loving-kindness towards myself and others became a crucial aspect of my quest for inner peace. Through meditation, I practiced sending love, compassion, and good wishes to myself, loved ones, and even those I found challenging.

By extending kindness and compassion, I discovered that I not only fostered inner peace within myself but also contributed to a more harmonious and peaceful world. This simple, yet profound practice transformed my relationships and allowed me to navigate the ups and downs of life with greater ease and grace.

Step 6: Surrendering and Letting Go

In the pursuit of inner peace, I learned the art of surrender. It involved letting go of the need for control and embracing the flow of life. I realized that peace could not be found in clinging to outcomes or resisting change. True peace arose when I surrendered to the present moment, accepting life as it unfolded.

Surrendering was not about resignation or passivity; it was about relinquishing the illusion of control and embracing the uncertainty and impermanence of life. By surrendering, I opened myself to the wisdom and guidance of the universe, trusting that everything would unfold as it should. This profound act of surrender brought me immense peace and freed me from the burden of trying to control every aspect of my life.

Conclusion:

Cultivating inner peace is a lifelong journey, an ongoing practice that requires dedication, patience, and self-compassion. Through mindfulness, gratitude, self-care, connection with nature, loving-kindness, and surrender, we can create a sanctuary of peace within ourselves. By nurturing our inner peace, we not only transform our own lives but also radiate that peace outwards, creating a ripple effect of serenity in the world around us.

Remember, the path to inner peace is not a linear one. There will be moments of turbulence and challenges along the way, but by committing to the practices outlined in this chapter, you will cultivate an unwavering sense of peace that will serve as a guiding light even in the darkest of times.

Embracing Authenticity

As I embarked on my journey of self-discovery and spiritual growth, one of the most profound lessons I learned was the importance of embracing my authentic self. It was a realization that led me to completely transform my life and unlock my true potential. In this chapter, I invite you to join me on this empowering path and explore the miracles that occur when we fully embrace our true essence in all areas of life.

Authenticity is not about conforming to societal expectations or trying to fit into molds that don't align with our true nature. It is about living in alignment with our core values, beliefs, and passions. It is about being true to who we are, without fear of judgment or rejection. When we embrace our authentic self, we unlock a sense of freedom, passion, and purpose that transcends all limits.

Embracing authenticity is not always easy. We live in a world that often puts pressure on us to conform, to be a certain way, and to meet certain expectations. From a young age, we are conditioned to believe that we should fit into predetermined roles and norms. We are bombarded with images and messages that tell us how we should look, how we should behave, and what we should aspire to. It is no wonder that so many of us lose touch with our true selves along the way.

But deep within us, there is a longing to break free from these limitations and embrace our uniqueness. There is a yearning to express our true essence and live a life that is aligned with our authentic self. It is this yearning that led me on a quest to rediscover who I truly am and live a life that is infused with purpose and meaning.

The journey of embracing authenticity starts with self-awareness. We must take the time to understand ourselves on a deep level. This requires a willingness to explore our thoughts, emotions, beliefs, and desires. It involves peeling back the layers of conditioning and societal expectations to uncover our true essence. Through practices like meditation, journaling, and introspection, we can begin to unearth the treasures that lie within.

Once we have a deeper understanding of ourselves, we must then have the courage to express our authentic self. This means being willing to show up as we truly are, without pretense or masks. It means owning our strengths, vulnerabilities, and unique gifts. It means honoring our truth and speaking our authentic voice. When we have the bravery to do so, we give others permission to do the same.

Embracing authenticity also requires us to release the need for approval or validation from others. We must realize that our worth does not depend on external validation but on our own self-acceptance and love. It is a liberating realization that allows us to be true to ourselves, regardless of what others may think or say. It is about trusting our own inner guidance and knowing that we are enough, just as we are.

Living authentically extends beyond our personal lives; it infiltrates every aspect of our existence. It means bringing our authentic selves to our relationships, our work, and our creative endeavors. It means infusing every interaction, every decision, and every endeavor with our true essence. When we do so, we not only experience a sense of fulfillment and joy, but we also inspire those around us to embrace their own authenticity.

Embracing authenticity is a lifelong journey. It is not a destination that we reach and then forget about; rather, it is a way of life. It requires ongoing self-reflection and a commitment to living in alignment with our true nature. But the rewards are immeasurable. When we embrace our authentic self, we tap into a deep well of wisdom, creativity, and joy. We experience a level of freedom and fulfillment that transcends any external circumstance.

So, I invite you to embark on this transformative journey of embracing authenticity. Take the time to explore who you truly are, accept yourself fully, and express your unique essence in every area of life. Embrace the miracle of living authentically and unleash your true potential. Remember, you are a unique and beautiful soul, here to shine your light in the world. Embrace your authentic self, and let your true essence flourish.

The Power of Service

Growing up, I was taught the importance of giving back to society. My parents instilled this value in me from a young age, and it was something I carried with me throughout my life. Little did I know that this simple act of service would have such a profound impact on my own personal growth.

One of the first experiences that stands out in my mind is when I volunteered at a local orphanage. I vividly remember the smiles on the children's faces as we played games, read books, and shared meals together. It was in these moments of genuine connection that I realized the joy of selfless giving. It wasn't about the material things or the hours spent, but rather the love and compassion that we shared. In giving to others, I discovered a sense of purpose and fulfillment that I had never experienced before.

As I delved deeper into my spiritual journey, I began to explore the various aspects of service. I became a certified life coach, using my skills and knowledge to guide others towards their own personal transformation. Through coaching, I witnessed firsthand the incredible power of service in helping individuals overcome their obstacles and find their true potential. The act of selflessly giving my time and energy to support others not only brought me immense joy but also strengthened my own sense of purpose.

In addition to coaching, I also delved into different healing modalities. I became certified as an Eden Energy Medicine practitioner, utilizing energy techniques to promote balance and well-being in others. The power of service was amplified as I witnessed the profound impact these modalities had on people's lives. Whether it was through energy healing, aromatherapy, or NLP, the act of giving brought about a transformative shift, enabling individuals to release emotional blockages and step into a place of empowerment.

One of the most powerful forms of service I have experienced is through breathwork. I have taken various breathing courses, each one delving deeper into the exploration of the breath as a medium for healing and transformation. Through the Science of Life & Breath, I learned how to harness the power of the breath to nourish and revitalize every cell in my body. The Dopamine Activated Breathing (DAB) course by Marcel Hof taught me how to tap into the breath to elevate my mood and enhance my overall well-being. And the Transcendental Meditation breathwork at the Pyramid Valley Institute allowed me to connect to a higher state of consciousness, experiencing profound inner peace and clarity.

But it was the Active Breathwork technique of Wim Hof that truly captivated me. This style of breathwork involves deep rhythmic breathing, followed by breath retention, and ultimately diving into the cold plunge. Through this practice, I discovered a newfound sense of fearlessness and resilience. It was in pushing my own limits, both physically and mentally, that I realized the transformative power of service on a deeper level. By embracing discomfort and stepping outside of my comfort zone, I was able to unlock a limitless potential within myself. I understood that service was not just about helping others but also about pushing myself to become the best version of myself.

Beyond the various healing modalities, I have also found solace in nature and physical activity. My love for trekking and hiking allows me to connect with the earth, immersing myself in its beauty and serenity. It is during these moments that I am reminded of the interconnectedness of all beings and the importance of service to the planet itself. By taking care of Mother Earth, we are ultimately taking care of ourselves and future generations.

As I reflect on my journey, I realize that the power of service extends far beyond the act itself. It is about cultivating a mindset of selflessness and compassion, and recognizing that giving to others is a gift in itself. Through service, I have discovered the true essence of who I am, finding fulfillment, purpose, and joy in the process. It has become a foundational pillar of my life, guiding my decisions, actions, and interactions with others.

My invitation to you, dear reader, is to explore the transformative power of service in your own life. Start by looking within and discovering your unique gifts and talents. How can you use these gifts to make a positive impact on those around you? It may be as simple as lending a listening ear to a friend in need or volunteering your time at a local charity. Remember, service is not about the grand gestures or the accolades; it is about the genuine desire to make a difference in someone's life.

And as you embark on this journey, allow yourself to be open to the lessons and growth that service brings. It may challenge you, push you outside of your comfort zone, and require you to confront your own limitations. But know that through this process, you will uncover your own inner strength, resilience, and potential.

The power of service lies not only in the impact it has on others but also in the transformation it ignites within ourselves. So, embrace the joy of selfless giving, and let the power of service guide you on a path of personal growth, fulfillment, and a deeper connection to the world around you.

The Role of Relationships

As human beings, we are inherently social creatures. We crave connection and thrive on the emotions and experiences that relationships bring. From the moment we are born, our lives are intertwined with others, starting with our parents, siblings, and extended family. These early relationships lay the foundation for our understanding of love, trust, and support. It is within the nurturing bond of family that we learn valuable lessons about empathy, compassion, and the power of unconditional love.

But as we grow older, we venture beyond the confines of our familial relationships and seek connections with friends, partners, and colleagues. These relationships, too, hold great significance in our journey towards fulfillment. They serve as a support system, a sounding board for our thoughts and emotions, and a source of inspiration and encouragement. In the words of the famous African proverb, "If you want to go fast, go alone. If you want to go far, go together."

One of the most profound lessons I have learned through my own relationship experiences is the importance of authenticity and vulnerability. In a world that often encourages us to wear masks and present ourselves in a certain way, it can be tempting to hide behind a facade. But true fulfillment can only be found when we open ourselves up fully to others and allow them to see and accept us for who we truly are. Building meaningful connections requires trust, mutual respect, and a willingness to let go of the fear of judgment. It is through these genuine connections that we can truly grow and evolve.

Another crucial aspect of relationships is the role they play in mirroring our own internal struggles and patterns. Have you ever noticed how certain people seem to trigger specific emotions or reactions within you, pushing your buttons in ways no one else can? These dynamics are not mere coincidences, but rather opportunities for self-reflection and growth. Our relationships serve as a mirror, reflecting back to us the aspects of ourselves that we may need to work on or heal. By examining our reactions and patterns within our relationships, we can gain valuable insights into our own behavior and make conscious choices to change and improve.

Relationships, however, are not always smooth sailing. They can be complex, messy, and filled with challenges. But it is precisely these challenges that offer us the chance to grow and evolve. In navigating the ups and downs of relationships, we learn essential life skills such as communication, compromise, and forgiveness. We recognize that conflict is not necessarily a sign of weakness or failure, but rather an opportunity for growth and deeper understanding.

In my own experience, I have found that it is in the face of adversity that relationships can truly thrive. It is during difficult times that the strength and depth of a connection are truly tested. We learn the true meaning of support, empathy, and love when we stand by each other's side in times of hardship. It is through these struggles that relationships can reach new levels of intimacy and trust, forging bonds that are unbreakable.

As I reflect on my journey towards fulfillment, I acknowledge the immense role that relationships have played in shaping me into the person I am today. The lessons I have learned, the growth I have experienced, and the love I have shared have all been deeply intertwined with the connections I have formed with others. Relationships have the power to bring us joy, fulfillment, and a sense of purpose. They teach us invaluable lessons about ourselves and the world around us. But above all, they remind us that we are never alone on this journey; that we are all connected in this intricate web of life.

In conclusion, I implore you to examine the role of relationships in your own journey towards fulfillment. Nurture the connections that bring you joy and support, and be willing to lean into the discomfort and challenges that arise. Cultivate authenticity, vulnerability, and open communication within your relationships, and allow them to serve as mirrors for your own growth and self-discovery. Embrace the power of relationships to bring fulfillment and meaning to your life, and in doing so, create a world filled with meaningful connections.

Embodying Gratitude and Abundance

Growing up in a middle-class family in Mumbai, India, I was taught the importance of material success and financial stability. My father and mother, one hard working entrepreneur and the other a loving homemaker, instilled in me the value of education and the pursuit of a successful career. And so, I followed their guidance and earned a bachelor's degree in Electronics Engineering.

But as I entered the corporate world, I realized that there was something missing in my life. I felt a deep emptiness, a longing for something more meaningful. Flashback, I met my soulmate, Neeta. I was 16 years old, and she was just 14. Little did I know then that she would become my anchor, my support system, and the driving force behind my spiritual awakening.

Neeta opened my eyes to a world of infinite possibilities. She introduced me to the concept of gratitude and abundance, teaching me that these qualities were not just elusive ideals, but tangible energies that could be cultivated within ourselves. Together, we embarked on a journey of self-exploration, determined to discover the secrets of manifesting our dreams and desires..

We continued to seek knowledge and experience in our pursuit of spiritual growth. I became a certified aromatherapist, using essential oils to enhance my well-being and promote emotional balance. I also trained as an NLP master practitioner, learning how to reprogram my mind to align with my true desires. Neeta, an ardent follower of Buddhism, always by my side, joined me in few of these endeavours, and supported me wholeheartedly.

However, it was our exploration of breathwork that truly transformed us. We attended an online course of transcendental meditation breathwork at the Pyramid Valley Institute, tapping into the ancient wisdom of the East. And, of course, As we ventured deeper into the world of spirituality, we realized that gratitude and abundance were not simply practices to be observed passively, but rather states of being that needed to be embodied. We understood that to attract more blessings into our lives, we needed to cultivate a mindset of gratitude and abundance on a daily basis.

So, we began our practice of gratitude. As we inculcated the habit of gratitude, we noticed a profound shift in our lives. Our challenges seemed less daunting, and our blessings multiplied. The more we expressed gratitude, the more blessings we attracted. It was a beautiful cycle that reaffirmed our belief in the power of gratitude to create abundance.

But embodying gratitude was not enough. We needed to cultivate a mindset of abundance as well. We realized that abundance was not just about material wealth, but about recognizing the abundance that already existed in our lives - the love, the friendships, the opportunities, and the growth.

To cultivate abundance, we practiced affirmative thinking. Instead of focusing on lack or scarcity, we trained our minds to see abundance in every aspect of our lives. We shifted our perspective from what we lacked to what we had, from what went wrong to what went right. This simple shift in mindset created a ripple effect, transforming our experiences and attracting more opportunities for growth and prosperity.

As I write these words, I am filled with a deep sense of gratitude and abundance. I look back on the journey that has led me here - the challenges faced, the lessons learned, and the love shared. And I know that everything I have experienced has brought me to this moment of realization - the understanding that embodying gratitude and abundance is the key to attracting more blessings into my life. It is a constant practice, a way of life that I continue to embrace as I strive to live in alignment with my higher purpose.

And so, I invite you, dear reader, to embark on this journey with me. Cultivate a mindset of gratitude and abundance, and watch as your life transforms before your very eyes. Embrace the blessings that are already present in your life, and know that more will come your way. Together, let us empower ourselves and take responsibility for our well-being on all levels of existence - physical, mental, emotional, and spiritual - so that we may truly enjoy life to its fullest.

<u>Living in Alignment</u>

Living in alignment requires a deep understanding of your values and beliefs. It is about discovering what truly matters to you and aligning your actions, decisions, and choices with those values. It is easy to get caught up in the pressures and expectations of society, family, and friends, but when you live in alignment, you prioritize your own values and make choices based on what feels right to you. This may mean making difficult decisions or going against the norm, but the rewards are worth it.

To live in alignment, it is crucial to have a clear sense of your true purpose. Your purpose is not just about having a successful career or achieving external goals. It is about finding your unique role in the world and making a meaningful contribution. Your purpose may evolve and change throughout your life, but the important thing is to stay connected to it and make choices that align with it. When you are living in alignment with your true purpose, you feel a sense of fulfillment and passion in everything you do.

Living in alignment also involves aligning your thoughts and emotions with your actions. It is about being aware of your thoughts and beliefs and choosing ones that support your goals and dreams. Negative thoughts and limiting beliefs can hold you back from living in alignment, so it is important to cultivate a positive and empowering mindset. This may involve practicing mindfulness, gratitude, and self-reflection to become more conscious of your thoughts and emotions.

Living in alignment requires taking responsibility for your own well-being on all levels - physical, mental, emotional, and spiritual. It is about prioritizing self-care and making choices that nurture and support your overall health and well-being. This may include eating healthy, exercising regularly, getting enough sleep, managing stress, and practicing self-care rituals that nourish your mind, body, and soul. When you take care of yourself, you are better able to show up fully in all areas of your life and live in alignment with your true purpose.

Living in alignment also means being true to yourself and expressing your authentic self in everything you do. It is about being honest with yourself and others, and not compromising your values or integrity for the sake of external validation or approval. It may mean setting boundaries, saying no to things that don't align with your values, and surrounding yourself with people who support and empower you. When you live in alignment with your authentic self, you attract people and opportunities that are aligned with who you truly are.

Living in alignment is a continuous journey. It is not a destination that you reach once and then forget about. It requires constant self-reflection, growth, and evolution. As you continue to uncover more about yourself and gain clarity on your true purpose, your definition of alignment may change. It is important to stay open, curious, and flexible, and be willing to adapt and make adjustments along the way.

In conclusion, learning to live in alignment with your true purpose and values is a transformative journey that leads to a life of fulfillment and meaning. It requires self-awareness, courage, and a willingness to prioritize your own well-being and authenticity. By making choices that are in alignment with your true self, you can create a life that is aligned with your values and brings you joy, peace, and a deep sense of fulfillment. Embrace the journey of living in alignment and unlock the potential within you to create a life that truly reflects who you are.

CHAPTER 7

EMBRACING THE JOURNEY

The Art of Self-Compassion

As I delved deeper into the realm of spiritual sciences, I realized that self-compassion is not just an abstract concept but an essential practice that can greatly impact our lives. It is the act of being kind and compassionate towards ourselves, embracing self-care and self-love.

Self-compassion is often misunderstood as self-indulgence or selfishness. However, it is far from that. It is about acknowledging our own suffering, treating ourselves with kindness, and providing ourselves with the care and understanding we deserve. It is about being gentle and forgiving with ourselves, just as we would with a loved one who is going through a tough time.

In our fast-paced and demanding lives, we often neglect our own needs and put ourselves last on the priority list. We push through challenges without giving ourselves the rest, care, and support we need to thrive. This lack of self-compassion can lead to burnout, stress, and even physical ailments. It is crucial for us to break this cycle and embrace self-compassion as an integral part of our well-being.

To cultivate self-compassion, we must start by changing our inner narrative. We tend to be our own harshest critics, constantly judging and criticizing ourselves for our perceived flaws and mistakes. It is time to replace this self-defeating dialogue with self-encouragement and understanding. We must learn to speak to ourselves in a kind and compassionate manner, offering words of comfort and love instead of harsh judgment.

Self-care plays a significant role in self-compassion. It involves taking care of our physical, mental, and emotional well-being. It means allowing ourselves to rest when we need it, nourishing our bodies with nutritious food, engaging in activities that bring us joy, and setting boundaries that protect our energy. Self-care is not a luxury; it is a necessity. By prioritizing self-care, we signal to ourselves and others that our well-being matters.

Self-love is another crucial aspect of self-compassion. It is understanding our own worthiness and valuing ourselves unconditionally. It is celebrating our strengths and accepting our weaknesses. When we love ourselves, we are better able to love and care for those around us. Self-love empowers us to set healthy boundaries, make choices that align with our values, and create a life that brings us fulfillment.

Practicing self-compassion may seem daunting at first, especially if we are accustomed to being self-critical or neglecting our own needs. However, with time and dedication, it becomes a natural and fulfilling way of life. Here are some practices that can help in cultivating self-compassion:

1. Mindfulness: Mindfulness is the practice of being present in the moment, without judgment. By tuning into our thoughts, emotions, and physical sensations, we can develop a greater sense of self-awareness and compassion. Taking the time to meditate, journal, or simply observe our thoughts can help us become more attuned to our own needs.

2. Self-Reflection: Regularly reflecting on our thoughts, actions, and emotions allows us to gain insight into our patterns and triggers. It helps us identify areas where we may need more self-compassion and areas where we can grow. Self-reflection can be done through journaling, therapy, or simply taking some quiet time for introspection.

3. Self-Forgiveness: We all make mistakes and have moments of weakness. Instead of holding onto guilt and self-blame, practicing self-forgiveness allows us to let go and move forward. Acknowledging our mistakes, learning from them,

and forgiving ourselves is an act of kindness and compassion.

4. Surrounding Ourselves with Support: Building a support system of friends, family, or professionals who uplift and encourage us is essential. Having people who remind us of our worth, offer guidance, and hold space for us to express ourselves is invaluable in cultivating self-compassion.

5. Self-Expression: Finding healthy ways to express ourselves, such as through art, writing, or music, can be cathartic and healing. It allows us to release emotions and connect with our inner selves. Through self-expression, we validate our experiences and nurture our authentic selves.

6. Gratitude Practice: Cultivating gratitude helps shift our perspective towards the positive aspects of our lives. By acknowledging and appreciating what we have, we can develop a sense of contentment and reduce the tendency to compare ourselves to others. A gratitude practice can be as simple as writing down three things we are grateful for each day.

7. Self-Compassion Affirmations: Affirmations are powerful tools in rewiring our minds and nurturing self-compassion. By repeating positive statements about ourselves, such as "I am worthy of love and kindness," "I am enough just as I am," or "I deserve to take care of myself," we reinforce self-compassion and invite more of it into our lives.

Remember, self-compassion is a journey, and we are all a work in progress. It requires patience, self-reflection, and the willingness to embrace our own imperfections. By learning to be kind and compassionate towards ourselves, we open ourselves up to a life filled with joy, fulfillment, and true well-being.

In the next chapter, we will explore the power of gratitude and how it can transform our lives. Stay tuned for a deep dive into the practice of gratitude and its profound impact on our mental, emotional, and spiritual well-being.

Cultivating Resilience

Growing up in India, I was always exposed to the concepts of resilience and perseverance. My father, who worked hard to provide for our family, instilled in me the values of determination and never giving up. They always encouraged me to embrace challenges as opportunities for growth rather than viewing them as setbacks. These early lessons shaped my mindset and prepared me for the journey ahead.

As I pursued my education and career in the field of marketing, I encountered numerous obstacles and setbacks. Whether it was struggling to find my place in a competitive industry or facing the pressures of meeting targets and deadlines, there were times when I felt overwhelmed and discouraged. But it was during these moments that I realized the power of resilience.

One of the key aspects of cultivating resilience is developing a positive mindset. Instead of dwelling on failures or setbacks, I chose to focus on the lessons they presented and the potential for growth. I recognized that every challenge was an opportunity to learn and improve. This shift in perspective not only helped me overcome obstacles but also allowed me to approach future challenges with a sense of empowerment.

Alongside developing a positive mindset, I also understood the importance of self-care and self-compassion in building resilience. Taking care of my physical, mental, emotional, and spiritual well-being became a priority. I realized that in order to bounce back from adversity, I needed to be in a state of balance and alignment. This led me to explore various healing modalities, such as energy medicine, aromatherapy, and meditation. Through these practices, I was able to cultivate a sense of inner strength and find solace during challenging times.

In addition to personal practices, I also sought support from my loved ones and mentors. Surrounding myself with a positive and uplifting community was instrumental in building resilience. Having people who believed in me and encouraged me to push through difficult times made a significant difference. Their support served as a constant reminder that I was not alone in my journey and that together, we could overcome any obstacle.

Throughout my exploration of resilience, I also came to understand the importance of embracing failure as a necessary part of growth. Failure is not something to be feared or avoided, but rather an opportunity for learning and growth. By reframing my perception of failure, I was able to overcome the fear of making mistakes and instead embraced them as stepping stones towards success. This mindset shift allowed me to take risks and pursue opportunities that I may have otherwise shied away from.

Another aspect of cultivating resilience is the ability to adapt to change. Life is full of unexpected twists and turns, and our ability to adapt to these changes determines our level of resilience. I learned that by embracing change and approaching it with an open and flexible mindset, I could navigate through life's challenges with greater ease. This adaptability not only helped me overcome obstacles but also opened doors to new opportunities and experiences.

Throughout my journey of cultivating resilience, I also came to realize that resilience is not a destination but a continuous process. It is an ongoing practice that requires dedication, perseverance, and self-reflection. Just like the muscles in our body, resilience needs to be exercised regularly in order to grow stronger.

In conclusion, cultivating resilience is an essential skill that allows us to navigate the challenges of life with grace and bounce back from adversity. It requires us to develop a positive mindset, prioritize self-care, seek support from loved ones, embrace failure as a part of growth, and adapt to change. Resilience is not something that can be built overnight, but rather a lifelong journey of self-discovery and personal growth. By consciously working on developing resilience, we empower ourselves to embrace life's challenges and emerge stronger, wiser, and more resilient than ever before.

The Power of Forgiveness

Forgiveness. A word that holds incredible power and yet seems so elusive at times. It is a path that many are hesitant to tread upon, as it requires us to confront our own pain and let go of past hurts. But what if I told you that forgiveness has the ability to set you free? That it has the power to heal wounds, mend broken relationships, and bring about a newfound sense of peace and liberation?

In this chapter, we will delve deep into the transformative power of forgiveness. We will explore the reasons why forgiveness is so crucial in our lives and learn techniques to let go of the burdensome weight of past hurts. This journey of forgiveness, though not easy, is an essential step towards our own personal growth and wellbeing.

I have come to realize that forgiveness is not an act of weakness, but rather an act of strength. It is a conscious choice we make to release ourselves from the shackles of resentment, anger, and hurt. It is not about condoning the actions of others or forgetting the pain they have caused us, but about liberating ourselves from the grip of negative emotions that hold us back from living a fulfilled and joyful life.

To embark on this journey of forgiveness, we must first understand the importance of forgiving ourselves. Often, we carry the weight of guilt and self-blame for past mistakes or regrets. We beat ourselves up, holding onto the belief that we are unworthy of forgiveness. But the truth is, we are all human. We make mistakes, we stumble, and we fall. It is in forgiving ourselves that we give ourselves permission to heal and grow.

Next, we must learn to empathize with the ones who have caused us pain. Understanding the motivations behind their actions can help us see the humanity within them. Perhaps they were hurting themselves, battling their own demons, or acting out of fear and insecurities. By acknowledging their struggles, we can begin to let go of the resentment and anger we hold towards them.

One powerful technique to aid in the process of forgiveness is the practice of meditation. Through meditation, we can cultivate a sense of inner peace and mindfulness. It is in this state of calmness that we can observe our thoughts and emotions without judgment. By acknowledging our pain and consciously choosing to let go, we can start the healing process.

Another technique that has helped me personally is the practice of writing forgiveness letters. These letters are not meant to be sent to the person who has hurt us, but rather to serve as a cathartic release of our emotions. In these letters, we can express our pain, anger, and disappointment, while also finding a way to forgive and free ourselves from the burden of carrying the weight of those emotions.

Additionally, I have found great solace and healing through energy healing modalities such as EFT (Emotional Freedom Technique) and TFT (Thought Field Therapy). These therapies involve tapping on specific energy meridians while focusing on the negative emotions we wish to release. This gentle tapping motion helps to release the emotional blocks and allows for a shift in our perception and ability to forgive.

One must also realize that forgiveness is not a one-time event; it is a continuous process. Just as our wounds need time to heal, forgiveness requires patience and persistence. It is important to honor our own healing journey and not rush the process. There may be days when we still feel the sting of the past hurts, but with each step we take towards forgiveness, we move closer to a place of wholeness and peace.

In conclusion, the power of forgiveness is unparalleled. It has the ability to mend broken hearts, restore relationships, and free us from the chains of resentment and anger. By understanding the importance of forgiving ourselves and empathizing with those who have hurt us, we open the door to immense personal growth and healing. Through practices such as meditation, forgiveness letters, and energy healing modalities, we can actively release our past hurt and embrace a life of joy, love, and freedom.

Remember, forgiveness is a gift we give ourselves. It is a choice we make to reclaim our power and live a life free from the burdens of the past. So, let go, forgive, and embrace the transformative power of forgiveness.

Embracing Change and Uncertainty

Learning to embrace change begins with a shift in perspective. Instead of viewing change as something to be feared, we can choose to see it as a chance to explore new possibilities and expand our horizons. Change is not the enemy; rather, it is the catalyst for personal and spiritual growth. By embracing change, we open ourselves up to new experiences and opportunities that might never have come our way otherwise.

But how do we begin to embrace change? How do we develop the courage and adaptability necessary to navigate the uncertainties of life? It starts with a willingness to let go of the past and step into the unknown. It means releasing attachments and expectations, and embracing the present moment with an open heart and mind.

One way to cultivate this mindset is through the practice of mindfulness. Mindfulness is the practice of bringing our full attention to the present moment, without judgment or attachment. Through mindfulness, we can learn to observe our thoughts, emotions, and sensations without becoming identified with them. This allows us to see change as it arises, without resistance or aversion.

In addition to mindfulness, cultivating a sense of self-awareness is crucial in navigating uncertainty. By developing a deep understanding of our values, strengths, and weaknesses, we can make more informed decisions and navigate change with confidence. Self-awareness requires honest reflection and a willingness to confront our fears and insecurities. It means taking the time to truly know ourselves and what we truly want in life.

Another important aspect of embracing change is developing a growth mindset. A growth mindset is the belief that we can always learn, grow, and improve. It is the understanding that our abilities and intelligence are not fixed, but can be developed through effort and perseverance. By adopting a growth mindset, we become more resilient and adaptable in the face of change. We see setbacks as opportunities for learning and growth, rather than as failures.

Cultivating a growth mindset also involves embracing discomfort and stepping outside of our comfort zones. Change often involves taking risks and trying new things. It requires us to face our fears and push beyond our perceived limits. But in doing so, we open ourselves up to new experiences and opportunities for personal growth. We discover that we are capable of more than we ever imagined.

In order to navigate uncertainty with courage and adaptability, it is also important to cultivate a sense of trust in ourselves and the universe. Trusting in ourselves means believing in our own abilities and intuition. It means having faith that we have the strength and wisdom to navigate any challenges that come our way. Trusting in the universe means surrendering to the flow of life and having faith that everything happens for a reason. It means embracing the unknown and trusting that it will lead us to where we need to be.

Learning to embrace change and navigate uncertainty requires practice and patience. It is an ongoing journey of self-discovery and growth. But by cultivating mindfulness, self-awareness, a growth mindset, and trust, we can develop the courage and adaptability necessary to navigate the ever-changing landscape of life.

As I reflect on my own journey of embracing change and uncertainty, I am reminded of the many times I have had to step into the unknown and trust in the process. Whether it was leaving the stability of a corporate job to pursue my passion for spiritual sciences, or facing personal challenges and setbacks, I have learned that change is not something to be feared, but rather something to be embraced.

Through my various healing modalities and spiritual practices, I have developed the tools and inner resources necessary to navigate change with courage and adaptability. I have learned to let go of attachments and expectations, and to trust in the wisdom of the universe. I have embraced discomfort and uncertainty, knowing that they are necessary for growth and transformation.

But perhaps the most important lesson I have learned is that embracing change is not a one-time event, but rather an ongoing process. Life is constantly throwing curveballs our way, and it is up to us to meet them with grace and resilience. By cultivating a mindset of growth, self-awareness, and trust, we can navigate the uncertainties of life and embrace change as a catalyst for personal and spiritual growth.

So, I invite you to embark on this journey of embracing change and navigating uncertainty with courage and adaptability. Open yourself up to new possibilities and allow yourself to be transformed. Remember, change is not the enemy; it is the doorway to a more expansive and fulfilling life. Embrace it, and watch as the possibilities unfold before you.

The Practice of Mindful Living

Have you ever found yourself caught up in the chaos of life, constantly rushing from one task to another, always thinking about what needs to be done next? Have you ever felt overwhelmed by stress and anxiety, unable to find a moment of peace? If so, you are not alone. Today's fast-paced world can easily consume us, leaving little room for self-care and reflection. However, there is a way to break free from this cycle, a way to bring balance and tranquility back into your life. It is the practice of mindful living.

Mindfulness, a concept rooted in ancient Eastern philosophy, has gained significant attention in recent years as a powerful tool for personal growth and well-being. It is the practice of being fully present and engaged in the present moment, without judgment. By incorporating mindfulness into your daily life, you can transform the way you experience yourself, others, and the world around you.

But how does one incorporate mindfulness into their daily life? How can we cultivate presence and enhance our overall well-being? The answer lies in creating simple, yet powerful rituals that anchor us in the present moment and remind us to be fully present in all that we do.

One of the most effective ways to cultivate mindfulness is through the practice of meditation. Meditation is about training the mind to focus and redirect our thoughts, allowing us to be fully present and aware. Finding a quiet space, sitting in a comfortable position, and closing your eyes, you begin to observe your breath. With each inhalation and exhalation, you bring your attention back to the present moment, letting go of thoughts and distractions. As you deepen your practice, you will notice that meditation not only calms the mind but also enhances your ability to be present throughout the day.

In addition to meditation, incorporating mindfulness into your daily life can be as simple as paying attention to the small moments and activities you engage in every day. For example, when you eat, take the time to truly savor each bite, noticing the flavors, textures, and sensations in your mouth. When you walk, feel the ground beneath your feet, the movement of your body, and the air caressing your skin. When you have a conversation with someone, be fully present, listening attentively and responding with intention.

Another powerful way to cultivate mindfulness is through the practice of gratitude. Take a few moments each day to reflect on the things you are grateful for. It could be something as simple as a warm cup of tea in the morning or the love and support of your family and friends. By focusing on what you have rather than what you lack, you shift your perspective and create a sense of contentment and appreciation for the present moment.

Incorporating mindfulness into your daily life also means being mindful of the things you consume, both physically and mentally. Pay attention to the foods you eat, choosing nourishing and wholesome options that fuel your body and mind. Be mindful of the media you consume, taking breaks from the constant barrage of information and connecting with nature or engaging in activities that bring you joy.

As you embark on the journey of mindful living, it is important to remember that mindfulness is a practice, not a destination. It requires commitment, patience, and self-compassion. Some days may be easier than others, but with consistency and dedication, you will begin to experience the transformative effects of mindfulness in your everyday life.

Incorporating mindfulness into your daily life can be the key to unlocking a deeper sense of presence, joy, and overall well-being. It is an invitation to slow down, to be fully present in each moment, and to cultivate a deep connection with yourself and the world around you.

As I continue my own journey of mindful living, I am reminded of the profound impact it has had on my overall well-being. It has allowed me to find a sense of inner calm amidst the chaos of life, to be fully present with my loved ones, and to appreciate the beauty and wonder of the present moment.

I invite you to join me on this journey of awakening, to incorporate mindfulness into your daily life and discover the transformative power it holds. Together, we can empower ourselves, cultivate presence, and enhance our overall well-being.

Are you ready to embark on this life-changing adventure? The choice is yours.

<u>Nurturing Authentic Relationships</u>

From a young age, I was exposed to the importance of deep connections and the impact they can have on our lives. This understanding only grew stronger as I embarked on my own journey of self-discovery and exploration. Along the way, I learned that authentic relationships are not just reserved for our romantic partners or immediate family members. They extend to all aspects of our lives, allowing us to create bonds that are built on trust, mutual respect, and genuine care.

Discovering the key elements of authentic relationships took time and effort. It required introspection, self-awareness, and a willingness to let go of preconceived notions about what a relationship should be. Through my studies and experiences, I uncovered three fundamental elements that are essential for nurturing authentic relationships.

The first element is self-awareness. Before we can truly connect with others on a deep and authentic level, we must first understand ourselves. This involves exploring our values, beliefs, and desires, as well as establishing boundaries and knowing our own limits. Through self-reflection and introspection, we gain a better understanding of our own needs and can approach relationships from a place of authenticity.

The second element is vulnerability. Authentic connections require us to be open and honest with ourselves and others. It means being willing to show our true selves, flaws and all, and allowing others to do the same. Vulnerability fosters trust and creates a safe space for deepening connections. By embracing vulnerability, we invite others to see us for who we truly are, allowing for more meaningful and authentic relationships.

The final element is active listening and effective communication. In our fast-paced and increasingly digital world, it can be easy to overlook the importance of truly listening to others. Active listening requires us to be fully present, to suspend judgment, and to genuinely engage with what the other person is saying. Effective communication goes hand in hand with active listening. It involves not only expressing ourselves clearly and honestly but also seeking to understand the perspectives and emotions of others.

Once we understand these elements, we can begin to cultivate deep connections with others. Authentic relationships are not built overnight but require continuous effort and commitment. It involves being present for others, offering support and empathy when needed, and celebrating their successes. Authentic relationships thrive on reciprocity, where both parties are invested in each other's growth and well-being.

But how can we apply these principles in our daily lives? It starts with being intentional in our interactions with others. It means taking the time to truly get to know those around us, to ask questions, and to actively listen to their responses. It involves being present, putting away distractions, and giving our full attention to the person in front of us.

Nurturing authentic relationships also means being willing to give and receive feedback. Constructive criticism is a vital component of growth, and when delivered with empathy and understanding, can strengthen our connections with others. It requires humility and a willingness to admit when we are wrong or when we have made a mistake.

Creating authentic relationships also involves recognizing and respecting boundaries. Each person has their own limits and comfort zones, and it is important to understand and honor them. Respecting boundaries shows others that we value and care for their well-being, fostering a sense of trust and safety within the relationship.

In this modern age, where technology has made it easier than ever to connect with others, it is crucial to remember the importance of face-to-face interaction. While social media and texting serve as convenient means of communication, nothing can replace the depth and authenticity that comes from engaging with someone in person. Meeting up for a cup of coffee, going for a walk, or simply spending quality time together can go a long way in cultivating meaningful connections.

As I reflect on my own journey of nurturing authentic relationships, I am reminded of the profound impact they have had on my life. These relationships have provided me with support and encouragement during times of difficulty, and have brought immense joy and fulfillment during moments of celebration. They have allowed me to grow and learn as an individual, and have empowered me to be the best version of myself.

In conclusion, nurturing authentic relationships is a lifelong journey that requires self-awareness, vulnerability, and effective communication. It involves being intentional in our interactions with others, respecting boundaries, and embracing the power of face-to-face connection. Authentic relationships have the power to enrich our lives and provide us with a sense of belonging and purpose. They remind us of the beauty and potential that lies within each of us, and inspire us to continuously strive for growth and self-improvement. So, let us embark on this journey together, embracing authenticity and cultivating deep connections with those around us.

The Power of Gratitude

Provocative Question: What if the key to unlocking abundance and happiness lies in something as simple as expressing gratitude?

As I sit down to write about the power of gratitude, it brings a smile to my face. The realization that something as seemingly small as expressing gratitude can have such a profound impact on our lives is truly astounding.

In my journey of exploring spiritual sciences and healing modalities, I have come to understand the immense significance of gratitude. It is not just a fleeting feeling of appreciation but a practice that can deepen and transform our entire existence.

I believe that gratitude is the gateway to abundance. When we practice gratitude, it shifts our perspective from scarcity to abundance, from fear to love. It is a subtle but powerful shift that plants seeds of positivity and attracts more blessings into our lives.

But how do we deepen our gratitude practice? How do we experience the true transformative power of gratitude in our lives? Allow me to share some insights and practices that have enriched my own journey.

1. Cultivate a Gratitude Ritual:

To deepen your gratitude practice, it is important to make it a regular part of your daily routine. Create a gratitude ritual that works for you. It can be as simple as writing in a gratitude journal every morning or evening, or taking a few moments before bed to reflect on what you are grateful for. The key is to make it a consistent practice that becomes ingrained in your daily life.

2. Go Beyond the Surface:

When practicing gratitude, it is easy to focus on the obvious things we are grateful for - our health, our family, our home. While these are indeed important blessings, deepen your gratitude practice by going beyond the surface. Take the time to appreciate the small everyday moments, the acts of kindness from strangers, the beauty of nature, the lessons learned from challenges. By acknowledging and appreciating even the seemingly insignificant things, we open ourselves up to a deeper sense of gratitude.

3. Express Gratitude to Others:

Gratitude is not just an internal feeling; it is meant to be shared. Expressing gratitude to others not only strengthens our relationships but also amplifies the energy of gratitude. Take the time to express your gratitude to the people in your life - a heartfelt thank you, a kind note of appreciation, a random act of kindness. By spreading gratitude, we uplift others and create a ripple effect of positivity in the world.

4. Practice Gratitude in Challenging Times:

The true test of our gratitude practice lies in how we navigate through challenging times. When we face hardships, it can be easy to slip into negativity and forget about gratitude. However, this is precisely when gratitude becomes most powerful. Look for the lessons and blessings hidden within the challenges. Find gratitude in the strength and resilience that emerges from difficult experiences. The ability to find gratitude even in the midst of adversity is a testament to the depth of our gratitude practice.

5. Embrace Gratitude as a Lifestyle:

To truly experience the transformative power of gratitude, it is important to embrace it as a way of life. Let gratitude permeate every aspect of your being and infuse it into your thoughts, words, and actions. When gratitude becomes a lifestyle, it becomes a magnet for abundance and joy. Embrace the attitude of gratitude in all that you do and watch your life unfold in beautiful and unexpected ways.

As I deepen my own gratitude practice, I am continually amazed by its power to shape my reality. The more I express gratitude, the more blessings I attract into my life. The more I cultivate a grateful mindset, the more abundance I experience. Gratitude has become the foundation of my spiritual journey, guiding me towards a more fulfilling and joyful existence.

So I invite you to embark on your own gratitude journey. Take a moment to reflect on all the things you are grateful for. Appreciate the miracles that surround you every day. Express your gratitude to yourself and others. Embrace gratitude as a way of life.

Deepen your gratitude practice and experience the transformative power of gratitude in your own life. Open your heart to the abundance that awaits you. Let gratitude be your guiding light on the path of self-discovery and empowerment.

Remember, the more gratitude you express, the more blessings you will receive. Embrace the power of gratitude and watch your life awaken to its true potential.

Living With Purpose and Passion

Living a life of purpose means understanding our unique skills, talents, and gifts, and using them for the greater good. It is about aligning our actions and decisions with our core values and principles. When we live with purpose, every aspect of our life becomes infused with a sense of meaning and intention.

For me, finding my purpose was a transformative journey. It required deep introspection, self-reflection, and a willingness to explore the depths of my being. I discovered that my true passion lies in the realm of spiritual sciences, and this realization has shaped the course of my life.

But finding purpose is only the beginning. Living with passion is what breathes life into our purpose. Passion is the fuel that propels us forward, gives us the energy to overcome obstacles, and pushes us to exceed our own expectations. It is the unwavering belief in the value and impact of what we do.

Living a life of passion means fully embracing the journey of self-discovery and personal growth. It means continuously seeking knowledge, expanding our horizons, and pushing the boundaries of our comfort zone. It means being open to new experiences, challenges, and opportunities that allow us to evolve and become the best version of ourselves.

One of the most rewarding aspects of living with purpose and passion is the immense fulfillment it brings. When we align our lives with our true calling, we find ourselves in a state of flow – a harmonious balance between our actions, thoughts, and emotions. It is in this state of flow that we tap into our full potential, experience deep joy and satisfaction, and make a meaningful impact on the world around us.

Living with purpose and passion also requires a sense of accountability and responsibility for our own well-being. It means taking charge of our physical, mental, emotional, and spiritual health. It means nurturing our relationships, cultivating a positive mindset, and prioritizing self-care. It is through this holistic approach to life that we can truly thrive and create a life of purpose and passion.

As I reflect upon my own journey, I can say with certainty that embracing purpose and passion has transformed my life in profound ways. It has allowed me to build a career that aligns with my true calling, to connect deeply with my soulmate, and to raise two beautiful children who embody the same zest for life. It has given me the courage to explore the mystical unknown, to delve into the depths of my spiritual self, and to continually seek knowledge and growth. And it has brought me immense joy, fulfillment, and a deep sense of gratitude for the blessings that surround me.

In closing, I urge you, dear reader, to embark on your own journey of self-discovery. Embrace your purpose, live with passion, and fully immerse yourself in the richness and beauty of life. It is through this transformative journey that you will uncover your true potential, experience profound joy, and make a meaningful impact on the world around you. Choose to live a life of purpose and passion, and let the awakening begin.

CHAPTER 8

CONCLUSION

Reflections on the Journey

Growing up in Mumbai, India, my life seemed to be on a set course. I had pursued a bachelors' degree in Electronics Engineering, followed by a Post Graduate MBA degree in Finance from the UK. But amidst the pursuit of a successful career in the marketing field, I felt a constant restlessness within me, an inner voice urging me to seek something more.

It was during this time that I met the person who would become my soulmate. She was only fourteen, and I was sixteen years old when our paths crossed. Little did I know that this meeting would change the course of my life forever. Our connection was instantaneous, and as we got to know each other, it became apparent that we were meant to be together. We shared a deep bond rooted in love, trust, and an unwavering belief in each other's dreams.

Fast forward a few years, and we found ourselves blessed with the arrival of two beautiful children - a daughter and a son. Parenthood brought new joys and challenges, and amidst the responsibilities of raising a family, my yearning for spiritual understanding only grew stronger. I realized that I needed to take ownership of my well-being on all levels - physical, mental, emotional, and spiritual - in order to truly enjoy life to its fullest.

And so, my journey into the realms of spiritual sciences began. I dived headfirst into various healing modalities and embarked on a path of self-discovery. I became a certified life coach, utilizing my knowledge and experience to guide and empower others on their own paths. I delved into the world of energy medicine, becoming an Eden energy medicine practitioner, harnessing the power of the body's subtle energies for healing and balance.

But my thirst for knowledge did not stop there. I sought out certifications in EFT (Emotional Freedom Technique) and TFT (Thought Field Therapy) to further enhance my ability to help others overcome emotional and psychological challenges. Aromatherapy became another facet of my healing journey, as I explored the intricate connection between scents and emotions. And as I delved deeper into the realm of the mind, I became a certified NLP (Neuro-Linguistic Programming) master practitioner, honing the power of language and perception for personal growth and transformation.

Yet, despite all these accomplishments, I saw myself as a work in progress. My spiritual thirst led me to explore various breathing courses, understanding the profound impact of the breath on our overall well-being. I underwent the Science of Life & Breath course by the Pratibimb Charitable Trust, discovering the profound connection between breath and the life force within. I embarked on the Dopamine Activated Breathing (DAB) course by Marcel Hof, opening my eyes to the power of breathwork in releasing stagnant emotions and facilitating inner healing.

I also delved into the world of Transcendental Meditation and breathwork at the Pyramid Valley Institute based in India, understanding the profound effects of conscious breathing on our state of mind and emotional well-being. And through the teachings of the Wim Hof method, I became an active breath practitioner, witnessing firsthand the transformative power of breathwork in enhancing physical strength and mental clarity.

Alongside my spiritual journey, I continued to nurture my other passions. I remained a fitness enthusiast, understanding the importance of caring for the physical vessel that housed my soul. I found solace and expression through playing the tabla and the guitar, immersing myself in the language of music. And the wonders of nature became a haven for me, as I found peace and inspiration in the beauty that surrounded us. Treks and hikes became a rejuvenating ritual, allowing me to connect with the earth and myself on a deeper level.

And now, as I reflect upon these years of exploration and growth, I am grateful for the lessons learned and the wisdom gained. It has not always been an easy journey, but it has been a deeply fulfilling one. I have come to understand that true empowerment comes from within, from taking responsibility for our own well-being and growth.

Through this book, I hope to inspire others to embark on their own transformative journeys. To delve into the depths of their souls, to explore the mysteries of the universe, and to unlock the incredible power that lies dormant within each and every one of us. This is not a quest for perfection but a journey of self-acceptance, self-love, and self-awareness.

So let us embark together, hand in hand, on this soul-stirring odyssey. Let us awaken to the incredible beings that we are, and let us embrace the infinite possibilities that await us. For the true power lies within our hands, waiting to be unleashed, waiting to transform our lives. The journey awaits.

Embracing the Unknown

From my early years, I have always possessed an insatiable thirst for knowledge and a deep longing to uncover the secrets of the universe. It was this burning desire that led me to pursue a career in marketing while simultaneously exploring the realms of spiritual sciences. As I delved into the depths of mysticism and ancient wisdom, I realized that the answers I sought could not be found in the confines of my textbooks or conventional knowledge. Instead, they lay hidden in the vast expanse of the unknown, waiting to be discovered.

With each passing day, I became more conscious of the infinite possibilities that lie beyond the veil of familiarity. It was not a mere acknowledgment of the unknown, but rather a conscious decision to dive headfirst into its depths that propelled my journey forward. I began to cultivate a mindset of curiosity, recognizing that in the face of uncertainty, lies the potential for immense growth and transformation.

Embracing the unknown is not about blindly stumbling in the dark, but rather about shedding the limitations of preconceived notions and opening oneself to new experiences. It is about acknowledging that life is an ever-evolving tapestry of possibilities, and instead of fearing the unknown, we must approach it with a sense of wonder and excitement.

In my quest for knowledge and self-improvement, I encountered various healing modalities and spiritual practices that further ignited my curiosity. I realized that the key to unlocking the infinite possibilities of the unknown lies in our ability to let go of control and surrender to the flow of life.

One of the most profound lessons I learned on this journey was the power of the breath.. Through focused breathwork, we can tap into our innate connection with the universe and unlock dormant potentials within ourselves.

Embracing the unknown also means relinquishing the need for certainty and control. It is a surrender to the divine orchestration of life, trusting that the universe has our best interests at heart. It requires us to let go of the fear of failure and embrace the knowledge that even in the face of uncertainty, we have the strength and resilience to overcome any obstacles that come our way.

As I reflect on my own journey of embracing the unknown, I am reminded of the countless blessings that have unfolded before me. From finding my soulmate at a tender age to raising two beautiful children, each step along the way has been guided by the unseen hands of the universe. It is through embracing the unknown that I have discovered the true essence of life – a never-ending symphony of possibilities, awaiting our participation.

In concluding this chapter, I urge you, dear reader, to embark on your own voyage of embracing the unknown. Cast aside the shackles of fear and skepticism, and embark on a journey of self-discovery. Embrace the unfamiliar with arms wide open, for it is within the vast expanse of the unknown that the true essence of life resides.

As I continue to tread this path, I am reminded of the words of Marcel Proust: "The real voyage of discovery consists not in seeking new landscapes but in having new eyes." With each passing day, my eyes become more attuned to the wonders that surround me, and my heart expands with gratitude for the infinite possibilities that lie before me. So, dear reader, I invite you to join me on this remarkable journey, with curiosity and openness as our guiding lights. Together, let us embrace the unknown and unlock the boundless potential that lies within us all.

The Power of Self-Exploration

Self-exploration is the process of delving deep into our own being, peeling back the layers of conditioning and societal expectations to discover our authentic selves. It is a journey that requires courage, curiosity, and a willingness to confront our fears and insecurities.

For many years, I had been living a life that others expected of me. As an accomplished marketing professional in the travel retail industry, I had achieved external success and financial stability. However, deep inside, I felt a sense of emptiness and dissatisfaction. I knew there was something more to life, something beyond the materialistic pursuits.

It was during this time that my curiosity for spiritual sciences began to grow. I immersed myself in books, attended seminars, and sought the guidance of spiritual teachers. I realized that true happiness and fulfillment could not be found in external achievements alone but required a deep connection with our inner selves.

With newfound passion and determination, I embarked on a journey of self-exploration. I started by questioning my beliefs, examining my thought patterns, and delving deep into my emotions. It was not an easy process, as I had to confront my fears, insecurities, and past traumas. Yet, with each step I took, I discovered a strength and resilience within myself that I had never known before.

One of the most powerful tools of self-exploration I discovered was meditation. Through this practice, I learned to quiet my mind, observe my thoughts and emotions, and connect with a deeper sense of inner peace and stillness. Meditation allowed me to detach from the noise of the external world and gain insight into my true desires and passions.

Another important aspect of self-exploration was embracing my unique talents and interests. I had always been passionate about music and had a natural inclination towards healing modalities. I realized that by exploring these interests further, not only did I experience joy and fulfillment, but I was also able to make a positive impact on others.

I began studying various healing modalities. Each certification brought me a step closer to understanding the intricate connection between the physical, mental, emotional, and spiritual aspects of our being.

But self-exploration is not limited to formal education or certifications. It is a continuous process of self-discovery and growth. It is about recognizing the patterns and habits that no longer serve us and replacing them with healthier alternatives. It is about embracing change and being open to new experiences and perspectives.

Through self-exploration, I discovered the power of breathwork. This not only helped me release stress and anxiety but also connected me to a deeper sense of vitality and aliveness.

In the process of self-exploration, I also discovered the importance of physical fitness and nature connection. I became a fitness enthusiast, engaging in activities like trekking and hiking. These experiences in nature brought me a sense of grounding, peace, and a deeper appreciation for the interconnectedness of all life.

As I navigated through the realms of self-exploration, I realized that it was a journey without an endpoint. It is a continuous unfolding, a never-ending quest to understand and align with our true nature. It requires courage to step into the unknown, to confront our shadows and embrace our strengths. But it is through this journey that we unlock our true potential and find lasting fulfillment.

I invite you, dear reader, to embark on your own journey of self-exploration. Look within, question your beliefs, and listen to the whispers of your heart. Embrace your passions, face your fears, and cultivate a sense of self-love and compassion. Recognize that you hold within you the power to create the life you desire, to find meaning and purpose, and to awaken to your highest potential.

May this book serve as a guiding light on your path towards self-discovery and empowerment. May it inspire you to embrace the power of self-exploration and unlock the limitless possibilities that lie within you. Remember, you are a work in progress, and in this journey, you will find the true essence of who you are.

<u>Continuing the Journey</u>

It is with this understanding that I feel compelled to inspire others to continue their own journey of self-discovery and personal growth. For I have come to realize that this journey is not a destination, but a lifelong process. It is not something that can be achieved and then forgotten about, but rather, it is an ongoing exploration of the self, of the world, and of the vast mysteries that lie beyond our current understanding.

Perhaps you, dear reader, have already taken the first steps on this journey. Perhaps you have already embarked upon the path of self-discovery, seeking to understand yourself on a deeper level, to unravel the secrets of your own soul. If so, I commend you for your courage and your commitment. For it takes great strength and determination to confront the shadows within ourselves, to face our fears and our insecurities head-on, and to embrace the truth of who we truly are.

But I also know that the path of self-discovery can be an arduous one, filled with obstacles and challenges that can sometimes leave us feeling lost or discouraged. It is during these moments, these times of doubt and uncertainty, that we need the most encouragement and support. We need someone to remind us that the journey is worth it, that the pain and the struggle are necessary for our growth and our evolution.

So let me be that voice of encouragement for you, dear reader. Let me remind you that the journey of self-discovery is not a straight line. It is not a clear and well-defined path that leads from point A to point B. Instead, it is a meandering and uncertain road, a series of peaks and valleys that lead us closer and closer to the truth of who we are.

Along this journey, you will encounter moments of profound clarity and insight, where the pieces of the puzzle suddenly come together and you see yourself and your life with a newfound clarity. These are the moments that make the journey worth it, that make the struggles and the challenges fade away in comparison to the beauty and the expansiveness of the truth.

But there will also be times when the path becomes clouded and obscured, when doubt and confusion creep in and threaten to derail your progress. During these times, it is important to remember that the journey is not about perfection or reaching some ideal state of being. It is about the process itself, the act of continually peeling back the layers and uncovering the truth that lies beneath.

In my own journey, I have found solace and guidance in the teachings of spiritual sciences. The study of ancient wisdom and the exploration of healing modalities have provided me with a framework for understanding myself and the world around me.

But I also know that the journey of self-discovery is not confined to any specific modality or set of practices. It is a deeply personal and individual process, unique to each person who embarks upon it. And so, while I can offer guidance and share my own experiences, ultimately, the journey is yours to navigate and explore in your own way and at your own pace.

To continue your journey of self-discovery and personal growth, it is important to cultivate a sense of curiosity and an openness to new experiences and ideas. Seek out teachers and mentors who resonate with your own values and beliefs, and be willing to learn from their wisdom and guidance. But also be willing to question and challenge the information and teachings that come your way, for ultimately, you are the expert of your own experience.

Embrace the unknown and the mysteries that lie beyond your current understanding. Allow yourself to be guided by intuition and inner knowing, trusting that the universe is conspiring in your favor. And above all, have patience and compassion for yourself along the way, knowing that growth and transformation often come with their fair share of messiness and discomfort.

As I bring my reflections to a close, I am filled with a renewed sense of purpose and excitement for the journey that lies ahead. For I know that the path of self-discovery is not a solitary one, but a journey that we all share, each one of us contributing to the unfolding tapestry of human consciousness. And so, I invite you, dear reader, to continue your own journey of self-discovery and personal growth, knowing that you are not alone, that there are others who have walked this path before you, and that together, we can create a more awakened and enlightened world.

So go forth, my friend, with courage and curiosity in your heart. Embrace the challenges and the uncertainties, for they are the catalysts for growth and transformation. And most importantly, never forget that the journey is not about reaching some final destination, but about the process itself, the continuous unfolding of who you are and who you are meant to be. May your journey be filled with wonder and joy, and may you always remember that the true beauty of life lies in the discovery of yourself.

Embracing Fulfillment and Enlightenment

As I delve deeper into the study of spiritual sciences and embark on this journey of self-discovery, I am constantly reminded of the importance of embracing one's path to fulfillment and enlightenment. It is through this pursuit that we can truly live a life of purpose and meaning.

In today's world, we often find ourselves surrounded by endless distractions and societal expectations that cloud our judgment and divert us from our true essence. We become consumed by the pursuit of material possessions, professional success, and external validation, all of which only offer fleeting moments of happiness. Real fulfillment, however, lies in something far more profound.

To begin this transformative journey, it is crucial to acknowledge and accept that we are not defined by our external circumstances or the opinions of others. Fulfillment is an inward journey, a deep dive into the realms of our own consciousness. It requires a shift in mindset, an awakening from societal conditioning, and a willingness to explore the depths of our being.

The path to fulfillment and enlightenment is unique for each individual, just as our fingerprints are unique to us. It begins by connecting to the source of our inner joy and aligning ourselves with our true purpose. For some, it may be the pursuit of creative endeavors, for others, it may be the practice of service and compassion. Whatever the path may be, it is essential that we listen to the whispers of our soul and follow the calling that resonates within us.

As I reflect on my own journey, I realize that embracing fulfillment and enlightenment is a continuous process. It is not a destination to be reached but rather a way of being, a state of consciousness that permeates every aspect of our lives. It requires us to be present in the here and now, to embrace the beauty of each moment, and to live with a sense of gratitude and appreciation. It is through this lens that we can find fulfillment even in the simplest of experiences.

In our quest for fulfillment and enlightenment, it is also essential to cultivate a deep sense of self-love and self-compassion. Often, we are our own harshest critics, constantly seeking perfection and striving to meet societal standards. However, true fulfillment lies in accepting ourselves as we are, with all our strengths and weaknesses. It is through self-acceptance that we can embark on a journey of self-transformation and growth.

It is my sincere hope that through this book, I can encourage readers to embrace their own path to fulfillment and enlightenment. I invite them to embark on a journey of self-exploration, to question societal norms, and to delve into the depths of their own being. It is through this courageous exploration that we can break free from the shackles of societal conditioning and embrace the true essence of who we are.

Living a life of purpose and meaning requires a commitment to both self-transformation and service to others. When we align ourselves with our true purpose, we become vessels through which love and compassion flow. We find fulfillment in contributing to the well-being of others and in making a positive impact on the world around us. In this interconnected web of life, the pursuit of individual fulfillment merges with the greater collective consciousness.

As I conclude this chapter, I invite you, dear reader, to embark on this transformative journey of embracing fulfillment and enlightenment. There is no greater gift than the realization of our own inherent divinity and the freedom it brings. Let us release the limitations of the past and step into the infinite potential that lies within us. Together, let us create a world where each individual lives a life of purpose and meaning, contributing to the collective flourishing of humanity.

The path to fulfillment and enlightenment awaits, dear reader. Are you ready to embark on this extraordinary journey? Let us begin.

Gratitude for the Journey

As I opened my eyes, a flood of memories washed over me. Memories of the transformative journey I had embarked upon, one that had allowed me to discover my true self and experience personal growth in ways I could never have imagined.

Looking back, it all began with a simple curiosity. I had always been intrigued by the mysteries of life, the spiritual realm that lay beyond the physical. While my career in marketing provided me with material success, it left me with a void. There was a thirst within me that could not be quenched by worldly achievements alone.

And so, I delved into the study of spiritual sciences, pursuing knowledge and wisdom with a fervent passion. I devoured books on ancient philosophies, attended seminars and workshops, and sought the guidance of spiritual masters. It was in this pursuit that I discovered the power of gratitude.

Expressing gratitude became a daily practice for me, a way to acknowledge and appreciate the blessings in my life. Each morning, I would write down three things I was grateful for, no matter how big or small. Through this simple act, I began to shift my perspective, focusing on the abundance in my life rather than the lack.

I realized that gratitude was not just about the things I possessed or the experiences I had, but about the lessons and growth that came with them. Every challenge, every obstacle, was an opportunity for me to learn and evolve.

With each hurdle I overcame, I became stronger, wiser, more resilient.

One of the most transformative experiences on my journey was meeting my soulmate. It was a serendipitous encounter, one that filled my life with love and joy. We grew together, supporting and uplifting each other through the highs and lows of life. Our children, a daughter and a son, were the embodiment of our love and the universe's gift to us.

My journey had taken me to places I never thought I would go. I began to approach each day with gratitude, embracing the challenges and setbacks as opportunities for learning. I learned to listen to my intuition, trusting the guidance it provided, and making decisions from a place of authenticity.

My love for nature became a vital part of my spiritual journey. The beauty and serenity of the outdoors allowed me to connect with a higher power, a force beyond comprehension. I would often embark on treks and hikes, immersing myself in the majesty of the mountains or the tranquility of a forest. It was in these moments that I felt the presence of something greater than myself, a reminder of the interconnectedness of all beings.

Through it all, I continued to evolve, embracing the role of a lifelong learner. I accepted that I was a work in progress, and that personal growth was not a destination, but a continuous journey. The more I learned, the more I realized how much there was to explore and discover.

Expressing gratitude for this transformative journey became a natural part of my daily life. It was a reminder of the blessings that had come my way, and the immense potential that lay within each and every one of us. I recognized that I had the power to create my own reality, to shape my life in alignment with my true purpose.

As I sat on the terrace, marveling at the beauty of the world around me, I couldn't help but feel an overwhelming sense of gratitude. Gratitude for the lessons, for the growth, for the love and joy that filled my life. It was a journey I would never trade for anything, for it had allowed me to awaken to my true self and to live a life of purpose and fulfillment.

And so, I continued on my path of self-discovery and personal growth, knowing that with each new day, there was an opportunity to learn, to evolve, and to express gratitude. For it is through gratitude that we are able to truly appreciate the beauty and abundance that life has to offer.

<u>Empowering Yourself</u>

It is with utmost sincerity that I implore you to take responsibility for your well-being on all levels of existence. Life is not something that happens to us, but something we actively participate in and co-create. The power to shape our reality lies within our hands, if only we choose to embrace it. That is the essence of empowerment - the recognition of our own agency and the conscious decision to wield it.

To truly empower ourselves, we must acknowledge that our well-being encompasses not only our physical health but also our mental, emotional, and spiritual states. These dimensions of existence are intricately connected, and neglecting any one of them can imbalance the others. It is only through nurturing and harmonizing these aspects of ourselves that we can truly enjoy life to its fullest.

On a physical level, caring for our bodies becomes paramount. Our bodies are the vessels through which we experience the world, and it is our responsibility to provide them with the nourishment, movement, and rest they need. Regular exercise, a wholesome diet, and sufficient sleep are not indulgences, but necessities for a vibrant and healthy life. By prioritizing our physical well-being, we lay the groundwork for all other areas of our existence to flourish.

However, it is not enough to focus solely on the physical. Our mental and emotional well-being are equally crucial for a fulfilling life. The mind, a powerful tool, can either be our greatest ally or our worst enemy. It is up to us to cultivate a positive mindset, to train our thoughts in a way that empowers rather than confines us. Self-awareness and mindfulness can help us identify and release negative thought patterns, allowing us to embrace a more optimistic and resilient perspective.

Likewise, tending to our emotional well-being is paramount. Emotional intelligence and self-compassion are skills that can be honed through conscious effort.

By acknowledging and validating our emotions, we cultivate a deeper understanding of ourselves and others. It is through this introspection and empathy that we can nurture healthier relationships, both with ourselves and those around us.

Yet, true empowerment extends beyond the physical, mental, and emotional realms. At the core of our being lies our spiritual essence, the essence that connects us to something greater than ourselves. This spiritual dimension, often overlooked or neglected, holds the key to our ultimate fulfillment. It is through the exploration and nurturing of our spirituality that we unlock our true purpose and meaning in life.

For me, the pursuit of spiritual sciences has been a deeply transformative experience. It has led me to explore various healing modalities, pushing the boundaries of what I once thought possible. I have delved deep into understanding the interplay between mind, body, and spirit. Through different breathing courses and healing techniques, I have unearthed the power of our breath as a tool for transformation, the healing energy held within our bodies, and the importance of aligning our thoughts and emotions with our desires.

It is this vast array of knowledge and experiences that I bring to you, dear reader. I am but a humble student on this journey of empowerment, forever a work in progress. My hope is that by sharing my own explorations and insights, I can inspire you to embark on your own path of self-discovery and empowerment. Together, let us take responsibility for our well-being on all levels of existence and embrace the fullness of life.

In the pages that follow, I invite you to explore the myriad tools, techniques, and practices that can support your journey of self-empowerment. From breathwork to meditation, from energy healing to positive affirmations, each chapter offers a gateway into a realm of infinite possibility. Remember, dear reader, that true empowerment lies not in passive reading, but in active application. It is up to you to take these teachings and weave them into the fabric of your own life.

As we embark on this remarkable adventure, let us approach it with open hearts and curious minds. Let us embrace the truth that we possess within us the power to create the life of our dreams. And let us remember that, in doing so, we not only empower ourselves but also inspire those around us to do the same.

The choice is yours, dear reader. Will you embrace this journey of self-empowerment and create a life of boundless joy and fulfillment? The power lies within you, waiting to be awakened. It is time to take responsibility for your well-being on all levels of existence and enjoy life to its fullest.

The Awakening Continues

I started this book with a simple intention - to share my knowledge and experiences in the hope of empowering others on their own paths of awakening. And yet, as I reflect on everything that has transpired, I am struck by the realization that there is so much more to explore, so much more to uncover.

Indeed, the awakening continues beyond the pages of this book, inviting readers like you to embark on a journey of self-discovery and personal growth. It is an open invitation to delve deeper into the mysteries of the universe and to question our very existence.

The first step towards continuing this journey is to acknowledge that we are all a work in progress. None of us have it all figured out, and that's perfectly okay. The awakening process is not a destination to reach but a continuous journey of growth and self-realization. It is a constant evolution and expansion of our consciousness.

In the pages of this book, I have shared various modalities and practices that have aided me in my own spiritual journey. From life coaching to energy medicine, from breathing techniques to meditation, each of these tools has the power to unlock new levels of awareness and understanding. But these are just the beginning.

To truly continue the awakening process, it is essential to explore further, to dive even deeper into the well of knowledge and wisdom that exists within and around us. We can do this by seeking out new experiences, by immersing ourselves in different teachings and philosophies, and by remaining open to the infinite possibilities that lie ahead.

Research has shown that the human mind is capable of incredible feats. It has the capacity to not only expand its knowledge but also to transform its very perception of reality. This means that as we continue our awakening journey, we have the ability to transcend our limiting beliefs and step into a reality that is more aligned with our true selves.

One of the tools I have personally found beneficial in this continued exploration is meditation. Through meditation, we can quiet the noise of the outside world and connect with our inner being. It is in these moments of stillness that we can tap into our intuition and gain deeper insights into our purpose and path.

Additionally, the practice of breathwork has also been instrumental in my journey. By consciously controlling our breath, we can access deeper states of relaxation and clarity. Breathwork has the power to release stored emotions, heal traumas, and expand our consciousness. It is a powerful technique that allows us to truly experience the interconnectedness of everything.

Beyond these practices, there are countless other avenues to explore. From ancient wisdom traditions to cutting-edge scientific discoveries, the possibilities are endless. Perhaps you may find solace in yoga or tai chi, or maybe you'll feel drawn to delve into the realm of sound healing or crystal therapy. The key is to listen to your intuition and follow your own unique path.

As the awakening continues, it is also vital to remember that this journey is not meant to be embarked upon alone. Seek out like-minded individuals who are also on this path of self-discovery. Connect with teachers, mentors, and guides who can offer support and guidance along the way. Share your experiences and insights with others, for in doing so, we create a ripple effect of awakening that expands far beyond ourselves.

So, as we reach the end of this book, I invite you to embrace the fact that the awakening continues. It is an ongoing process that unfolds with each passing day. Trust in your own inner guidance, have faith in your ability to navigate the unknown, and above all, be open to the wondrous possibilities that lie ahead.

I am humbled and grateful to have shared this part of my journey with you. But this is just the beginning. The true power lies within you, waiting to be unleashed. Embrace the journey, explore the depths of your being, and allow the awakening to continue, unearthing new dimensions of existence that you may never have imagined.

The path may be winding, and at times challenging, but the rewards are immeasurable. As you step into the unknown, remember that within you lies the spark of divine consciousness, waiting to illuminate your way. Embrace your power, for the journey of awakening is a magnificent and sacred gift that continues beyond the pages of this book.